21 LEADERSHIP LESSONS OF NARENDRA DAMODARDAS MODI

VIJAY JHINDAL | NITIN AGARWAL | PANKAJ SHARMA

GRAPEVINE INDIA

Grapevine India Publishers Pvt. Ltd.
Plot No.4, First Floor
Pandav Nagar
Opposite Shadipur Metro Station
Patel Nagar
New Delhi - 110008
India
grapevineindiapublishers@gmail.com
contact@grapevineindia.com

Printed and bound in New Delhi

FOREWORD

Narendra Modi.

The name in itself ignites a 1000 emotions. I choose the word 'ignite' carefully, because if India has woken to a 1000 dreams, if the Fire in the Indian Belly to achieve something extraordinary has to be re-kindled out of its Hibernation mode, the one single catalyst that assumes the credit is Narendra Modi. Period. And NOW starts a new period!

A period where we Indians will learn to believe in our aspirations under the invigorating leadership of NaMo. He is the Man who is building the 'Platform of Confidence' on which we gain the courage to dream that our dreams will just not remain dreams but will become a reality.

"Confidence is the First Requisite to Great Undertakings" said Napoleon & every Indian, no matter where he/resides India or Abroad, will overwhelmingly agree that it is refreshing & inspiring to witness an Indian Prime Minister have the confidence, conviction & most of all, the immense courage to actually 'spell' out his vision & dreams about India & Indians. Most will agree that unfortunately Policy-Paralysis has been a salient feature in Governance (or lack of it) in recent times & therefore a Visionary like NaMo with a uncluttered mind that's enlightened with fresh new courageous ideas & endeavours will work wonders for all of us.

In this 21 century, 21 leaderships styles of Modi and many more continue to inspire us.

~ Babul Supriyo, Singer, Actor,
Union Minister, Government of India

महेश गिरी
सांसद, लोक सभा
पूर्वी दिल्ली संसदीय क्षेत्र
सदस्य :
स्थायी समिति – शहरी विकास मंत्रालय
परामर्शदात्री समिति – पर्यटन एवं संस्कृति मंत्रालय

MAHEISH GIRRI
Member of Parliament, Lok Sabha
East Delhi Parliamentary Constituency
MEMBER :
• Standing Committee on Urban Development
• Consultative Committee on Tourism & Culture

MPED-5126/NASP 29-12-2014

Dear Nitin & Pankaj,

21 leadership lessons on Narendra Modi is a book that encapsulates the synchronization between traits of leadership, communication, history and nationalism.

Narendra Modi is viewed and worshipped not only as a dynamic and efficient leader but also as a brilliant orator, who matches his words with his actions and his actions with his words. In this book, the idea of comparing his leadership styles to the 21 topmost leaders of all time can only be seen as a fair and appropriate articulation of his outstanding and exceptional leadership and administrative skills.

He is undoubtedly the most popular leader in today's world as he manages crisis as they occur, identifies opportunities and takes avid risks, taps the youth on social media and markets the true essence of India in a way no leader has ever done before. It is an absolute honor and privilege to serve the nation under his supervision and guidance.

Yours Sincerely

Maheish Girri

Maheish Girri

C-330, BALAJI MANDIR ROAD, VIVEK VIHAR, PHASE-1, DELHI-110095
Tel.: +91-9289837837, -+91-9289303030, +91-11-22145366 • E-mail : contact@maheishgirri.com

PRAISE FOR THE BOOK

"An ideal book to understand our prime minister's leadership qualities. He is a very capable person and possess all qualities of a statesman but the system which he has inherited is a stumbling block. Any robust system is built in centuries, which didn't happen in India."

~ Dr. Udit Raj, MP, Lok Sabha

"Narendra Modi is an Indian success story on a titanic scale, leaping from selling tea to becoming chief minister of his state to the primeministership of India, winning a majority in the Lok Sabha for the BJP through concentration on defined goals and the selection of methods and personnel who can achieve. This book explains some of the reasons behind Modi's success, and by its insights into his functioning indicates why the odds are that Prime Minister Modi will replicate his success in Gujarat on a national scale. The book helps others to use elements of the unique "Modi methods" to their advantage"

-Prof M D Nalapat
UNESCO Peace Chair and Director, Geopolitics and International Relations Department at Manipal University

CONTENTS

Along Paths Not Taken

Floating a sea of uniformity
Uniqueness often shot down
Overrated and dismissed by those
With no vision
Of what the future could be

Fear of change and what it means
Raises its loud voice
Above the noise
An unknown road less travelled
May lead to riches beyond compare

Out of place among the suits
Buttoned up and neatly pressed
All trimmed and primed
An image of perfection
Perception is the reality

A different voice arises from the crowd
A way unheard, a cry alone
Leaders emerge when least expected
From those who challenge the paradigm
Seeing visions of promise and purpose
Along paths not taken

~Mark Schutter

INTRODUCTION

Who is a leader and what differentiates him from others? Does he do things differently? Does he do different things? Is he a creation of situations or is he creator of situations? Are leaders made or do they posses some inborn traits?

These questions indeed have been boggling human mind since ages. Historians, management gurus, and preachers have their own methods to define the concept of leadership, narratives on leaders and their traits, which many a times may be pristine while at other times, they could be hazy or chaotic.

While there could be multiple ways to discuss the genesis of leaders, one thing that surely speaks about them is that they possess a charisma of thoughts and vision which attracts the people around them.

People follow them for their vision and mission, which otherwise is not present in others. They emulate their vision, mission and ambitions and become part of the stride that the leaders take.

We all know that humans by nature are social animals who feel most comfortable in their herds. Apart from the flight of personal and social ambitions, history is filled with examples of great leaders who were the by-products of chaos and challenges that society was passing through. These leaders emerged in that chaos and guided people through it.

So to fight the might of British empire (about which it was said that the sun never set over it), a frail person by name of Gandhi stood up to catch the fancy of his followers with his unique concept of non-violence; to challenge the ills of apartheid, an obscure Nelson Mandela took the shackles against the might of a white regime; a young Greek named Alexander, driven by his passion to reach the East, stood on the shores of Indus and claimed to have cobbled the world's biggest empire.

What is common among them is that all of them had some traits which resulted in them being classified as leaders.

As the Bhagwat Gita said:

"Leaders should embrace rather than avoid formidable challenges because they bring out the leaders' greatest strengths.

Leaders should be resilient in their actions and should not be weakened by pain and pleasure.

Selfish desires and animosity obscure the purpose of leadership.

Leaders achieve lasting power and glory by exercising compassion and selfless service.

Effective leaders do not lead by fear or anger.

Character is core to effective leadership.

Leaders need to be aware of the self and the surroundings."

All of them had a desire to take the formidable challenges. They were resilient in their action by remaining focussed on their goals. Despite personal ambition, the drive to move ahead was more social than personal. They protected and mentored their believers and followers alike, they were fearless and strong and above all, highly conscious of their own position and that which was around them. hile political leaders are most recognised and appreciated due to their relative societal impact, leadership as a trait can be displayed in any field and domain.

When we conceptualised this book, the biggest challenge for us was defining the realms of leadership and discovering traits of leadership. We chose a unique number 21 to enumerate upon these traits.

The number 21 has a great mathematical and mythological connotation.

Its mathematical uniqueness lies in the fact that

21 is the smallest number of distinct squares needed to tile a square. Further, the sum of numbers on a dice also numbers 21 (1+2+…6). The square as a figure is considered to be the most harmonic figure of all mathematical figures and further, the figure originates from a set of lines which are not just parallel but also equal (that explains why a square root is a number multiplied by the number itself). It represents duality and thus, 21 can be called as the smallest harmonic unit to be present among the numbers.

In the Hindu mythological sense, number 2 represents duality of nature (Parush and Prakriti); Parush symbolising life, effort, vigour and ambition (all traits of a great leader) and Prakriti implying environment and situations (again a defining factor for leaders to emerge). The number 1 on the other end symbolises Brahaman or consciousness and self (an important trait for a successful leader).

Hence, we chose 21 as the number of traits to define leadership traits of any individual.

The second challenge was identifying global leaders who displayed these 21 traits. It would have been easier if we had chosen just one individual; like our protagonist Narendra Domodardas Modi, and then tried to connect the dots. But we wanted to take it to the next level by choosing not one, but 21 different leaders, so the matrix became that of 441 instances, a rather large number to address.

Next was tracing those traits in our protagonist Narendra Damodardas Modi, whose rise to power and life in itself presents a unique example. Born in a rather modest family, Narendra Modi's rise to the top political post in the world's biggest democracy is a unique example, which to a large extent speaks about the Indian democracy in itself, whereby any person can reach the top pedestal through sheer hard work and political opportunities being thrown upon him. His rise within his own party cadres from being a simple Rashtriya Swayamsewak Sangh Pracharak to first, as a Chief Minister of Gujarat and then as Prime Minister, presents a fitting story of leadership displayed by him. As stated earlier, looking at it from the lens of multiple perspectives was a challenge in itself, as the comparative benchmarks for ascertaining his leadership traits varied in the historical time, spanning from Napoleon to Martin Luther King to Ronald Reagan, cultural differences in context of those leaders, the pursuant political situations and others. We were looking for specific traits displayed by both Narendra Modi and those leaders and viewing it from the context of those traits.

While many stories could have been simple underdogs or dark horses in the context of people rising to great heights, Narendra Modi's story was not a straight-jacket tale of a common man rising to great heights, but his strategic thinking coupled with foresight and technological impetus presents a contemporary story and a modern context of how a leader should think in present times. Unlike many of his benchmarks who might have enjoyed certain unique propositions, Narendra Modi's rise is also an interesting tale intermingling personal, professional, technical and social ethos and then using the opportunities thrown to emerge as a people's leader.

His story is also of great relevance as he has been a disruptive force in Indian politics in many ways. It's not just his political or administrative pedigree but also the manner in which his rise has impacted the Indian politics, which more or less faced a rather long era of notional political instability (in majority due to the coalition politics) for 30 years, before transcending back to political stability with Narendra Modi leading his party to an absolute majority. The political turnaround is a significant phase in Indian polity as it rearranges the pegging of political force with the main opposition party - the Indian National Congress - for the first time in Independent India, getting marginalised at national level. Further, the trend of regional parties was often seen as a by-product of rising regional aspirations struggling for survival. So what did Modi do to rise and become a national leader and what in him caught the fancy of a common Indian was something worth deliberating.

There have been multiple books which have been

written on Narendra Modi post his win and even otherwise, but most of them are commentaries of either his political work or his biographies or news-based works. No work indeed tried to move beyond the obvious and decipher those traits which can indeed be learning traits for not just political leaders but for leaders across the board.

The key question was whether these traits were unique to Modi, or at some point, someone somewhere displayed those traits in the past. The question was an important one in solving the puzzle, not from the perspective of whether or not Modi displayed those traits knowingly or unknowingly, but more from the perspective of identifying those traits. The point of commonality was an important aspect of this work, which is more of a leadership book than a simple story of a protagonist.

As stated earlier, there existed a wide cultural, political or situational difference among the stories and examples, but the common ground was the trigger-response system which led to situations under which Narendra Modi responded in the same manner as these global leaders. The traits in themselves established the common ground for defining what is leadership and what traits leaders display when they are faced with similar consequences. It's important to state that many of these traits are indeed ingrained in the very personality of these leaders and they effectively used these traits to forward their agenda and vision.

Narendra Modi's rise from the small town of Vadnagar to becoming Prime Minister is also an interesting story itself, as it presents a classic example of personal passion, grit and dedication, coupled with pursuant opportunities that created these stories. Considering that India is the world's largest democracy with a billion plus population who is politically and emotionally charged, it always remains an inherent challenge for prospective aspirants to compete against a larger pool. Modi's rise is also significant because turbulence and systematic opportunities for him were limited for him to rise, unlike other leaders with whom he has been compared, many of whom indeed displayed the qualities either due to systematic opportunities in the form of fight for freedom, or had slightly better power positions like being at the top positions in their respective hierarchies. Modi didn't have any such advantage on his side and hence his rise is closer to people who had similar situations (like Barack Obama, in some sense).

Modi's ascent has also been a controversial one in majority due to his ideology and mannerisms, which sometimes could be a challenge for leaders looking for universal appeal. However, the duration of his sustenance as a leader (first as Chief Minister for three tenures and now emerging as the Prime Minister) thus spoke something about his strength that merged his administrative calibre with a great futuristic imbibing of technology and communications tools. His rise, thus, could not be called as a simple, one-time aberration but a deliberate and sustained long-term strategy of reaching to the highest pedestal of power. Narendra Modi presents a contemporary definition of leadership and how leaders could emerge and sustain. It is a fitting treatise on the very concept of leadership and its discourse.

1 | Clarity of Vision

"To grasp and hold a vision, that is the very essence of successful leadership." ~ Ronald Reagan

History proves that one of the intrinsic traits of any great leader is him being a visionary. While we all have a vision of something or the other, a great leader not only has a vision but also has the trait of transferring his vision to people around him so that it becomes an organisational or a social vision. As is said, people don't follow people but people follow an idea of achievement. When Alexander set his foot on the lands of Asia and defeated the mighty king Darius III of Persia with an army of handful soldiers, the achievement was not just hailed as his own but was projected as a Greek supremacy over the world, though this could only have been achieved for Alexander had a clarity of vision to become a global conqueror.

Similarly when Gandhi picked up a dollop of salt from Dandi or called for Quit India, his vision of free India was resonated with all, for it reflected his single minded agenda of a free India. His acts were not just seen as singular acts but part of the larger plan of freeing India from the clutches of Britishers.

An important aspect of defining one's vision is that it is unambiguous and simple. Often, leaders of all kinds fall prey to ambiguity and complexity. What needs to be understood is that vision is not a compilation of flowery words which appear good on paper and words, rather it's the base upon which one lays the foundation of implementation. A simple vision, thus, is not just clear and focused but also conveys a distinct message as to what needs to be achieved by following that vision.

A vision is not just a dream of the leader's objective. Rather, it also serves as a guiding post to the people who look up to that leader and defines the path that needs to be adopted to achieve that vision.

Having a clear vision of how one wants the future orientation to be, is perhaps the most important leadership quality. A leader in whom the masses have placed their trust naturally has the power to influence and it thus becomes his great responsibility to project a clear vision of what he is working for. This helps provide direction, meaning, enthusiasm and a grand sense of success for all those who are part of that milieu. Clarity breeds understanding; understanding breeds productivity and productivity breeds confidence which in turn breeds desired returns.

Coming out as the most popular leader of the masses of Independent India, Narendra Modi succeeds in projecting himself as a man with a clear sense of purpose. It is not just the highly appealing propaganda he shares, but also confidence in his dream of a developed India focusing on inclusive growth and better governance. His apparent long-term, 'complete' vision is what sets him apart as a leader with power to bring and manage the much-needed change that India needs. Millions of Indians have trusted him with this immense responsibility, and that is because Modi was confidently able to display a future image of India, along with sound ideas and schemes to bring that vision to reality.

While campaigning in the Indian General Election 2014, Modi's party, Bhartiya Janta Party (BJP) seemed to be the only one with a defined vision. Even the election campaign goal was clear: attaining at least 272 seats to have majority votes. This vision, in order to be effective, was communicated well in advance to the party as well as the public, by launching it under the name 'Mission 272'. Effective leaders have this appealing capability to attract followers by giving them something to strive for. In the present times, the people of India desperately *wanted* change for the better, having been left bamboozled by the

Government so far. Selecting Modi to represent them at the highest level had a lot to do with his clarity as to the right way forward for India.

Most would agree that in the decades preceding Modi, India lacked a clear vision for growth and development. Development was often confused with either populist schemes or subsidies based models. The economic model and the governance structure were either oriented towards established populism or managing the Collation Dharma, thus, people in general lacked a clear vision of growth. Modi provided a clear dream in the form of change which is not generic in nature but touched upon specific agendas.

In an even broader perspective, his dreams for India can be taken into account to serve as broad examples of what lies behind his motivation. He seems to have thought of every major aspect that he believes needs attention, in order to make India truly shining. Encompassing an extensive range, his vision includes everything from fostering agricultural research to developing quality infrastructure to financial investments. The focus is on urbanization, education, bringing down corruption and inflation, creating jobs, skill development, use of technology for effectiveness, and doing everything with an inclusive approach. His 'Brand India' idea, that professes development in the five T's: tradition, talent, tourism, technology and trade, also helped generate an image of an India that proudly stands at par with developed economies of the world. Modi gives the example of China, looking at how development of new cities led to their economic prosperity. This idea greatly appeals to the public, especially industrialists, who are quite appreciative of a politician talking about development of infrastructure. The Ambani brothers, among the leading industrialists in India, called Modi "a king among the kings", appreciating his grand vision and purpose.

Modi's vision is not just well articulated but also well systematised with all actions taken or projected by him leading back into a single objective of "Making India Great". This connection helps his target (the citizens of India) to remain connected with his vision. So when he speaks of better roads, better technology, better governance, every citizen of India sees that it's imperative for making India great. An important aspect of his vision is also to give a benchmark for vision. He speaks about great global nations like Japan and China and how they have emerged as leaders, thus defining the final goal of India to be in the same league. He has a good grasp of entire governance system of India, as ruling a state for 15 years has given him a good understanding of grassroots challenges and thus his vision imbibes grassroots issues in same the breath as national or international issues. His vision is not just a by-product of a dream which may sound frivolous to achieve, but has a solid base of understanding, limitation and clear path of implementation.

As Theodore Hesburg, President of University of Notre Dame, USA, stated, "The very essence of leadership is that you have to have a vision. It's got to be a vision you articulate clearly and forcefully on every occasion." Similarly, Narendra Modi reflects upon his vision at all occasions. This reiteration over time has got deeply embedded not just in mind of Narendra Modi himself but also of the people who have reposed faith in him.

From day one Modi has projected an agenda of development which makes him a representative on which people can pose in their faith for development. He has constantly and evidently hammered the concept of development so much so that the vey mention of Narendra Modi now equates with growth and development. This is an important trait for any leader and his leadership message.

This single minded agenda and clarity has indeed been beneficial for him for through this he has warded off and shifted the political discourse towards his own agenda of growth. While his critics challenged his regional credentials or ideological affiliations they could never question his administrative abilities or his vision, which thus played an important role in diffusing his critics and paving a greater connect with his desired stakeholders.

His vision doesn't go by as sham, for he has effectively managed to communicate his ideas about achieving these goals. Through his well-articulated speeches, he has displayed his ideas behind India's economic development, corruption-free government and what he means by his idea of 'Minimum Government, Maximum Governance'. Part of what makes him identifiable to the people is his stark detection of problems plaguing the country and its economy. So when a leader professes meaningful solutions to help resolve issues people can associate with, he is the one where the trust of the masses is placed, as is the case of Narendra Modi.

Tracing back to Modi's early life, parallels can be drawn to his present and his persistence on defining a vision before moving forward. As a child when Modi started attending the daily Shakha organized by RSS, he was perhaps looking for a refuge from the physical bondage of his home life. He is known to have been in search of a distinct identity right from the beginning, drawn in by the discipline and different life of RSS, also being greatly inspired by the authority exhibited by the RSS leader.

Narendra Modi is an exemplary example of a leader with a vision. However, it is important to note that this trait isn't nurtured overnight. One might not have that sense at all, especially when one is young and yet to explore the world. In the midst of his later years as a teenager and a young adult, Modi too was gripped with non-clarity and confusion about life. Since he was a dedicated worker, he was able to explore his strengths and understand the ways of the world, which helped him develop his own vision for himself. He was never ashamed of performing even the least important tasks, because he had simply to reflect on his long-term vision and know that those were just stepping stones to a better and more powerful future.

Considering the example of Gujarat, where Narendra Modi served as Chief Minister from 2001-2014, it is apparent what a well-defined vision can do. His plans, created well in advance for the future, are so detailed and well-formulated that they are good enough to serve Gujarat till 2030. The changes brought into the state with his policies have brought in investments in Gujarat, which has led to its impressive development. In order to promote investments in Gujarat, Modi also initiated 'Vibrant Gujarat', held by the Government of Gujarat as a biennial investors' summit. Modi has visualized Gujarat to emerge as a nodal centre in Asia, to serve as a common platform for countries like China, Japan, Thailand and Sri Lanka.

This is part of the grander vision that Modi created for the state of Gujarat, what came to be called as the 'Gujarat Model'. This model for development has been effective in certain aspects and helped bring about impressive changes in Gujarat, making it one of the top economically growing states in India. Be it agricultural improvements or industrial expansion, Modi had it all laid out in clear terms, what they aim to achieve and how they plan to implement their ideas. This is probably the greatest reason that the vision came to reality. The agri-GDP growth registered during the 2000s saw agriculture in Gujarat growing by 9.8% per annum, compared to the meagre 2% during the 1990s.

As Narendra Modi takes charge of the country as Prime Minister, laying out his vision for India, there's hope and a certain level of confidence that India will be on the right path to achieve its ideal state. He has vowed to end corruption, make India a manufacturing hub and enable financial and digital inclusion. Modi's clarity of vision is further indicated by the segmentation of overall goals into smaller, precise goals, which makes it easier to understand where we're heading. Example, when Modi states that he aims for a 'Clean India', he makes it look achievable by providing a timeline (by 2019) and by organizing campaigns (like hosting the World Toilet Summit in Delhi) and providing government support (allocating increased amount of money for toilet construction). Similarly, to achieve his aim of a technologically savvy and inclusive country, Modi has come up with ideas such as the Digital India mission, aimed at transforming India into a digitally empowered knowledge economy. Just like a super-magnet, Modi's clarity of vision draws him relentlessly forward.

An important trait that has been displayed by the vision of Narendra Modi is that it not just epitomises the vision of modern India but is deep rooted within Indian culture and what our forefathers envisioned. His vision has a unique characteristic of transcending into every aspect of Indian mind-set from basic cleanliness to technical expertise to becoming a global power and as it is simple to comprehend by the common masses. Hence, they imbibe the vision as their own.

Footsteps - Dhirubhai Ambani

Great leaders who have scaled global heights have proved to be stimulated by a larger vision of who they want to become. Their goals are distinct, which helps them stay on track and focus on the right things. One such example of a leader with the persistence on having a clear vision and ideas is business tycoon and founder of Reliance Industries, Dhirubhai Ambani. A man ahead of his times, he dared to dream on a boundless scale, which is something Narendra Modi also symbolizes. Dhirubhai converted Reliance from a small trading house to a large private sector group, listed among *Fortune's* 'World's Top 500 Companies'. This tremendous growth was possible because of his belief in having a larger than life vision.

Modi's distinct ideas about India's growth and development are parallel with how Dhirubhai imagined the country to be. Convinced that India could become an economic superpower, he wanted Reliance to contribute towards this ideal. Both these leaders understood the importance of investment as a driving tool for development. While Dhirubhai was among the first to discover and believe in the untapped potential of capital markets, Modi has also been emphasizing on generating investments and improving basic infrastructure.

Dhirubhai believed in going forward with your vision in mind, but also emphasized on the importance of 'keeping with the times'. Updating those grand plans with new inputs and taking developments into account, is equally important. This is reflected in Modi as he charts out plans and goals, adopting new practices and revising them to accept what is the most relevant. Just as Dhirubhai, starting off with a humble beginning, created a life backed by exceptional achievements, Modi symbolizes what it means to follow one's vision with confidence, courage and conviction.

An Important similarity between these two leaders is also that both charted a path on their own and overcoming a challenge from established circles. Their vision had a jest of creativity as they discovered newer methods to achieve their objectives. While operating in an overtly protected regime, Dhirubhai could have chosen the path of his contemporaries who were too concentrated in protectionism and secured markets offered to them. Rather, he chose to tap the opportunities of today with a vision for tomorrow. The big business houses of then invested little in R&D or skills or even becoming globally competitive. Many of them thus fell out when the Indian market opened in 1991. Dhirubhai's vision was not just short term, aimed at profit of today but also long term - becoming globally competitive. Similarly Narendra Modi's vision is not short term, oriented towards achieving smaller improvements in the governance framework, but is long term - making India globally competitive. Both of them formed a unique mix of top-down and bottom-up approach of vision implementation.

In the eighties, Reliance established the Patalganga refinery in record time, which was not just a remarkable business feat but a world class facility to refine petro products at the cheapest price. This was a feat with a vision for future, for Dhirubhai knew that someday or the other when India will be forced to open its markets, then Reliance should be numero uno. He thus undertook investment for the future decades ahead of a change. Similarly, Narendra Modi with his target of reaching at the top post started engaging at national level since 2002-2003. Sensing the weaker points of BJP in South India, he started visiting those states from 2002-2003 with his speeches being translated in local languages and media interviews being carried in local newspapers. Similarly in most important states of Uttar Pradesh and Bihar (which cumulatively send the largest number of MPs in Indian Parliament) he started engaging with grassroots cadres. Though it was only a decade later that his name was propped for the top post, yet his long term vision and investment garnered great returns for him with Uttar Pradesh and Bihar returning close to a third of all BJP MPs in the parliament of 2014.

Another point of similarity between the vision of both Dhirubhai and Narendra Modi is its strong economical connect. While one can attribute this to their famous Gujarati genes, yet the vision of Dhirubhai to create value proposition for his shareholders and that of Narendra Modi to put development and economic benefit to citizens at large as the base are indeed closely connected and reflective of each other. Coming from rather humble backgrounds, both understood the fact that true prosperity and larger social or organisational benefits could only be achieved if economic benefits percolate to the lowest strata of their stakeholders. This approach made them obvious leaders upon whom people and shareholders at large could place their faith.

These leaders are accomplished not because they harbour special characteristics, special surname or familial ties, but because they choose to make their lives special. They dare to dream big, have a vision in mind and sincerely work towards realizing that vision.

2 | Perseverance and Determination

"Our greatest glory isn't never falling, but rising every time we fall. ~ Oliver Goldsmith

Challenges, setbacks, hurdles: almost everyone faces them, especially those in a position of power and responsibility. What differentiates good leaders from exceptional ones is not their intelligence or affinity for good strategies, but their self-determination. In times of challenging circumstances, brilliant ideas are necessary, but the leader's perseverance and will to get through the problem is something far more fundamental and important. Imagine what would happen if the leader of a group turns around and vanishes, abandoning his team! That certainly won't be a pretty picture.

Effective leaders have the resolve to look at problems

with a brave face. Thinking calmly and staying in control leads them to manage and look for possible alternative solutions. A perseverant leader, driven by a constant vision, is able to make his team anchor on his beliefs, thoughts, values and principles. It helps one to stay motivated.

Narendra Modi's journey from a *bal sevak* in RSS to the Prime Minister of India is a story of deep-rooted determination. Set with a vision in mind, he has been looking into solutions and working on them persistently. His zest for work was quite visible and in a lot many instances, appreciated. In the early 1990s, Modi was handed the responsibility of L K Advani's Rath Yatra (1990) and Dr Murli Manohar Joshi's Ekta Yatra (1991-92) despite being in a junior role in the state unit in BJP. The RSS leaders had quickly provided their assent taking into consideration Modi's initial years of success and hard work.

Given the fact that the Indian political system is characterised by issues of groups and favouritism where the emerging and struggling political aspirants will spend more time in pleasing their seniors than working at grassroots levels, Narendra Damodardas Modi chose the path of hard work to make his mark, despite being aware that achieving success and admiration through work and results is a long path vis-à-vis any short cut.

His desire to achieve the unachievable, pushing him

to extreme and social awareness played an important part in overall rise of Narendra Modi. People who know Modi from earlier days recount him as a self-motivated and socially conscious individual who followed high morality in his personal disposition. Indeed many of his old associates find that Modi has displayed a unique trait of incrementing his perseverance and determination as he kept moving upwards in power hierarchy. He is known as one who never basks on his past or present glories, but has his sights set on the next milestone even before achieving the previous one.

As a youngster, Modi seemed to be interested in disassociating himself from his small life in Vadnagar. As a means of escape from his family life, he 'disappeared' for stretches of time to spend time completely by himself in a secluded place. Really wanting to do something that would give him a distinct identity, Modi never gave up. Perseverance became the prerequisite to living the life he wanted to live.

Starting small and performing jobs lower in class is usually something that is not preferred, unless the individual harbours a broader perspective and like Modi, knows that those are just stepping stones for future success. People tend to give up, feeling dejected at the quality of work required of them, sometimes giving up because of jealousy. Successful people who go on to become leaders sometimes start no different, but they are quite willing to overcome challenges and have the strength and determination to see their goals churning into fruition. Modi's jobs and responsibilities during his initial years in RSS can be described as menial and routine. However, Modi's idea of carrying out all tasks effectively prepared him for the various roles he was later asked to play. Certainly, no job is useless!

This also helped him later in his career as it provided people the confidence in his abilities and his determined will to passionately work for the cause he believed in. The reason the RSS was handing out bigger responsibilities to him was because they were pleased with his efficiency and the fact that he performed whatever he undertook with utmost enthusiasm. When such individuals go on to become leaders, and are responsible for a lot many people, it is this determination settled in them that allows them to keep on pursuing their goals and in the process, leverage things to their advantage. In the midst of any crisis, they must have the capacity to continue.

As Modi rose up the ranks, he found that his Dharmic rooted perspective needed a modern reinvention. In order to keep himself up with the times, he understood and valued the importance of having a broader perspective. Although there would be evidence and opinions for the otherwise, one can't deny the fact that he did try learning from whatever he could and inculcating modern management principles that are so necessary to lead India in the contemporary scene.

It's not that Modi didn't face failures or challenges; in fact, leading Gujarat during the Gujarat Riots and Godhara issues became a hounding issue for him. Surely, no leader would want to be held responsible for such an issue, especially when he took command of a state only months back. Anyone who is even remotely aware of the Indian governance system would appreciate that the system is rather complex and not as simple as it appears. The strong hold of regional political satraps, bureaucracy and the established power centres with the Indian political framework provides little leverage for even the established Chief Minister of any state to operate, more so when one is new and just acclimatising himself with the complexities of governance. However, despite all the negativities that surrounded him, Narendra Modi chose to concentrate and shift the discourse to the economic agenda and growth which doesn't suffer from the normal discrepancies of secular v/s non secular, regionalism, etc. He's remained perseverant that the only model that Gujarat and he would propagate is purely economic, which in the end would benefit all. Though his critics kept hitting him with the phrase, 'single agenda', he chose to respond to them with a vibrant economic model. He provided a never-thought-of model of investment inflow, with senior IAS officers being assigned to and accountable for every investment flowing within the state. His detractors and critics not just challenged him in India but ensured that even his international reputation remains challenged; however, with a single minded focus on his state, he carved a path of economic diplomacy where the international investors themselves pushed their respective governments to remain engaged with him. Probably this is one of the few instances where international diplomatic efforts were targeted towards a particular state of India and not just at national level.

Another example that displayed his determination and perseverance was the handling of the devastations that occurred in the Gujarat earthquake in 2001, which killed more than 20,000 people, destroyed 4,00,000 houses and accounted for a loss of billions in economic damages. The incident occurred around nine months before Narendra Modi took the reins of the state. Modi could have chosen to just maintain the continuity of efforts, but after becoming the Chief Minister, he galvanised investment and rehabilitation efforts to such an extent that today, Kutch boasts of one of the finest models of rehabilitation across the world and the area is economically better than what it was before the tragedy.

It is said that Alexander the Great, unlike other kings of past, never remained hidden by his cavalry or artillery, rather he would stand with his front-line soldiers and lead the attack from the front. Similarly, Narendra Modi is not known to remain contended by just delegation of duties to either his colleagues or officers but prefers a more hands-on approach of remaining at the forefront in testing times.

The heights great men reached and kept were not attained by sudden flight, but they, while their companions slept, were toiling upward in the night. ~ Henry Wadsworth Longfellow

In the most recent scenario, Modi's win as Prime Minister of the country in May 2014 is in itself a valid example of the results of being consistently persistent. Emerging as a symbol of hope for the youth of this country, Modi shoulders the expectations of the people and reflects their unwavering confidence in his leadership abilities. Continuously stating the government's goals and plans, not just to his team but to the media and the public, he has generated that sense of confidence that things can turn out to be good. His apparent determination to make it happen also helps motivating the team, which further works with a positive attitude.

Organizing hundreds of rallies all over the country in an unimaginable time period, being at the forefront of all his initiatives, making full use of technology and social media to leverage his party, Modi carried out all possible ideas to win his quest for Prime Minister. Modi has also generated criticism and times of uncertainty in the face of problems. There's enough evidence to see the number of issues he has had to deal with, most of which were a direct attack to his pride, something he keeps safe and sound. Ram Jethmalani, senior politician and eminent lawyer, started his article in the Sunday Guardian with these lines: "No politician in independent India has been demonised in such a relentless, Goebbelsian manner as Narendra Modi, and no politician has withstood it with as much resilience and courage as him, notwithstanding the entire Central government, influential sections of the media machinery and civil society arraigned against him."

It requires tenacity to be able to conserve one's emotions and maintain clarity as to the goals. Narendra Modi is one such person, strong and courageous, with fortitude to carry on in the face of insoluble dilemmas.

Narendra Modi has displayed a high level of personal initiative, perseverance and a will power to counter all odds no matter what they are, and he in many ways epitomises what Gurdev Rabindra Nath Tagore wrote in his famous poem Ekla Chalo Re (Go All Alone)

Jodi tor dak sune keu na ashe, Tobe ekla cholo, ekla chalo, aekla chalo re, Aikla cholo re (If no one answers your call, then walk alone, be not afraid, walk alone my friend)

Jodi kue kotha na koe, ore o re o obaghaga, keu kotha

na koe Jodi sobai thake muhk phirae, sobai kore bhoye, Tobe poran khule, O tui, mukh phute tor moner kotha, Ekla bolo re (If no one talks to you, O my unlucky friend, if no one speaks to you, If everyone looks the other way and everyone is afraid, then bare your soul and let out what is in your mind, be not afraid, speak alone my friend)

Jab kali ghata chaye, Ore o re o andhera sach ko nigal jaye, Jab duniya sari, dar ke age sar apna jhukaye, Tu shola banja, Wo shola banja, Jo khud jal ke jahan raushan karde, Ekla jalo re. (When dark clouds cover the sky, When darkness engulfs the truth, When the world cowers and bows before fear, You be the flame, The flame that burns you and banishes darkness from the world, be not afraid, Burn alone my friend)

~ Gurudev Rabindra Nath Tagore

Footsteps - Mahatma Gandhi

The difference between what we do and what we are capable of doing would suffice to solve most of world's problem

~ Mahatama Gandhi

Great leaders have attained success and fulfilled their goals; be those personal or for the welfare of society or the country, primarily because of the inherent abundance of determination. Mahatma Gandhi, the visionary who was an integral figure in India's fight for independence, is also an example of sheer perseverance and will power. Gandhi advocated non-violence, believing in fighting for the truth with *ahimsa*. The term *satyagraha* coined by him literally means "persistence of truth" and goes on to show how perseverance was a factor deeply ingrained in him, not just in his actions, but also in his every belief.

Before jumping into the independence struggle of India, Gandhi undertook a country-long journey to understand the challenges that lay in front of him. He knew that India is a diverse country and to sew it into a thread of single agenda would require sheer determination and hard work. During the freedom struggle, Gandhi would often travel to remote areas to remain ingrained with the people at large. He was determined that until and unless he covers India in its entirety, he could neither emerge as a national leader nor could push ahead his agenda of its independence. Similarly, much before Narendra Modi set his sights on the national pedestal, he had started travelling to states that were weak points of his party. He knew that while he was successfully leading his home state Gujarat, his larger agenda of national growth could only be achieved if he emerged as a national leader upon whom people of all states and regions could repose their faith. Even during the 2014 general elections, he travelled far and wide across India covering the entire length and breadth of the country to remain in connect with the masses at large. His determination to achieve the goal can be adjudged by the very fact that he would begin his day as early as 4 AM in the morning and after his daily chores would conduct back to back election meetings across India, sometimes on same-day flying from Gujarat to North East and then to South India and parts of North India and returning back to Gandhinagar to grab a sleep of 2-3 hours daily. This perseverance and focus indeed resulted in Narendra Modi becoming a national leader and people across the board connecting with him and propagating his agenda at large.

Gandhi knew that the path to India's freedom was long but he was also determined that no matter what he would not shun the path of non-violence, so much so that he suspended the *satyagraha* movement when a police station was set ablaze in Chauri Chaura, a town near Gorakhpur in present day Uttar Pradesh. He felt that it's important to first spread the real meaning of *ahimsa* and then move forward in implementing it with the masses. Gandhi's approach thus was oriented towards first spreading the vision and then laying the foundation for its implementation. Similarly, Narendra Modi feels that that true growth of India could only be achieved if it is linked to economic growth of masses. In an articulate manner he has conveyed his vision to the countrymen and now he is working determinedly to untangle the bottlenecks that lie in front of him and his vision.

One reason why effective leaders persevere is their conviction in their own beliefs. Gandhi was sure of non-violence as the right means of winning freedom and although he was widely criticized by other leaders, he was quite set in his belief and was determined to make India free by those means. He spread his message far and wide, worked at the forefront, motivated and mobilized the people and despite many setbacks and despicable circumstances, never gave up. Narendra Modi shares this quality with Gandhi, who created his plans and points of action based on the ultimate goal in mind, and carried it out with strong-founded determination. Such leaders place a 'never say die' attitude in the midst of their minds and continue working to achieve their goals with complete focus. Be it his career cycle, or the vision he has now set for India, Modi has provided enough evidence to believe that he would see it through, no matter what.

Even as a youngster, Gandhi looked for opportunities to learn from everywhere he went, especially during his stay in England when he was studying law. When he faced roadblocks, he did not simply try to return to India however much he wanted, but decided to stay back and look for alternative solutions to resolve his problems. Just like Gandhi's persona exuded his perseverance, Modi's stance also reveals him to be someone who would not easily give up. His authoritarian nature might even add to this determination, for he would work towards achieving what he promised with utmost diligence so as to maintain his authority and trust in the people. Gandhi's unrelenting pursuit of his goals, self-abnegation, courage, tolerance and perseverance are qualities Narendra Modi seems to have picked up and is now using to become an effective leader.

3 | Humility

"A great man is always willing to be little."
~ Ralph Waldo Emerson

One of the greatest leadership qualities, humility is the virtue of having a modest and humble opinion of one's own capabilities and self. Leaders who harbour humility within themselves come across as respectful of others, courteous and have a ready acceptance for all kinds of people. Humility is sometimes quite underrated because many people have this misconception of humility being parallel to softness, making a leader seem weak and easy to dupe. In reality, it is anything but.

Great leaders recognize the importance of being patient and humble and duly incorporate this quality within them. They understand the fact that they're being looked upon by their followers and teams. Accepting that they alone cannot possibly achieve all the goals set before them, they generate an attitude of humbleness. Such leaders, whether in teams or families or organizations or countries, don't come across as arrogant or full of themselves. They attribute success to not just their own capabilities, but to their teams. They admit their mistakes and appreciate ideas when they come from others. Such people create an environment of openness and comfort. Jim Collins, the influential consultant and author, mentioned in his book *Good to Great* that in his assessment of the top-performing companies, he found leaders to have an abundance of humility. They shared credit for success and were the first ones to accept blame for mistakes.

Even though Narendra Modi as a person sometimes gives the impression of being overly proud, he does have a sense of respect for others. Keeping aside his habit of throwing sarcasm towards other political parties, Modi is relatively known to be grateful and patient towards others. Nilanjan Mukhopadhyay in his book *Narendra Modi: The Man, The Times* wrote about his experience when he went to interview Modi. He feels that in an era when political leaders cohabit with journalists, treating and flattering them because of the power of media in their hands, Modi's warmth towards him had a personal touch. He didn't seem affected by the journalist's associations or opinions or what he wrote; his choice of words, overall body language and expressions touched a personal chord.

Leaders make themselves accessible in this manner. A boss who dominates over his subordinates, never appreciates or acknowledges them and constantly emanates an aura of arrogance is hardly someone who'd be approached, even in the face of an impending crisis. More than anything else, a good leader needs humility to survive as a desired leader for a long period of time. Narendra Modi might be a believer in this notion, and perhaps has inculcated this quality since childhood. Modi is a man with humble beginnings: his middle class family life, his early start in RSS where he as much as cleaned the floors and prepared breakfast, his youth when he helped his father and uncle run tea stalls. Although filled with a zest for power and authority, Modi has an understanding of a humble life and thus has an element of consideration for others.

An important ingredient of humility is the manner in which one treats others. Be it someone lower in power and status or someone who helped one rise, one must be ready to appreciate them. Sometimes being humble and easy to approach has also been mistaken for timidity. It takes one to cultivate a broad mindset, especially a leader with power, to be able to see things from a bigger perspective. Approachable leaders who appreciate their team members and acknowledge their inputs are better able to retain them. This also increases their productivity, apart from making the leader more in touch with the ground problems surrounding them.

Modi has also been a person who greatly respects his teachers, mentors and elders, as well as keeping his word to those whom he made promises. One such instance is in the year 2001, when he had been invited to his school's Golden Jubilee function by his childhood friend, then principal of the school. Modi, not wanting to break his word, rushed to Vadnagar from an important national programme in Wagah Border. After his speech at the celebrations, his teachers came forward with garlands for him, but Modi refused to accept those, stating instead that it is the teachers who actually deserve the garlands. Even during his initial years in the RSS, he was respectful of those elder and wiser to him. The Jana Sangh's organizing secretary Nathalal Jhagda was someone with whom Modi had forged a close relationship. Modi is known to have been personally tending to the secretary: dropping and receiving him from railway stations and carrying his luggage for him.

In another incident dating back to 1990, two Indian Railway Traffic Service Probationers, both women, were travelling in train from Delhi to Ahmedabad. Since their waitlist tickets hadn't yet converted, they were asked to share seats with two young BJP politicians for some time. During the course of a good conversation and a hearty meal for which the younger man paid, they discussed politics and history. When the Travelling Ticket Examiner couldn't find them seats, the two men readily gave up theirs and slept on the floor instead. Leena Sarma, one of the two women wrote about this incident in an article published in *The Hindu*, originally published in an Assamese newspaper in 1995. She had scribbled down the names of those two men: Shankersinh Vaghela and the younger one, Narendra Modi.

Humility also borders on authenticity. Modi seems to understand this and whether intentionally or not, he has created his public image as a grateful person and someone who, with utmost manners, respects other people. When he was elected Prime Minister of India in May 2014, Modi in his acceptance speech struck a note of humility. He said, "I want to say that you have chosen leaders, I want to request my countrymen that you have given 60 years to a leader, now give 60 months to a servant." Having this sense of humility for the people and the country is something that makes Modi a desired leader.

Trusting others and handing them responsibilities is also an effect of a humble attitude. Delegating duties and authority encourages subordinates to contribute their own ideas as well. Allowing them to make decisions boosts their confidence, which is what Modi has also done. In his regime as Prime Minister, he asked almost all cabinet ministers to assign substantial responsibilities to their junior ministers, holding the diktat that seniors shouldn't hold all administrative matters. Dealing with pride is a struggle for many leaders, as is with Modi, but one can't deny that he doesn't try.

An important trait in Narendra Modi that differentiates him from other leaders is that he has maintained his humility and never fell prey to power flowing off in one's own mind. Often it has been seen that as one moves higher in the sphere of influence, one is susceptible to fall prey to this trait where gradually one trades off humility with arrogance. This is displayed by an insignificant, yet an important act when Modi, after becoming the Prime Minister, came to know that a peon's son in his office has cleared civil services exam. He invited both father and son for tea and spent some quality time with them. In most cases, Indian leaders of all kinds are so enamoured in their own self that they would care least for anyone who is not influential or not economically beneficial to them, but here is a Prime Minister who not only is aware of a grade IV employee of his staff but also goes out of way to give them a preference and sparing time from his busy schedule.

Another important incident that displays his humility is that with every win in Gujarat as a Chief Minister, he would visit his elders and seek their blessings. In fact, once Keshu Bhai Patel, his one-time mentor floated a new party on the eve of state elections of

Gujarat when Modi came back to power with thumping majority as Chief Minister. Modi made his first visit to Keshu Bhai's house to seek his blessings. Many a people who know him state that Modi maintains a fine discipline of humility and personal touch which many a times seems missing in people in power. He boasts of a sharp memory and on several occasions would go an extra mile to recognise and appreciate efforts of people around him.

It's an evident fact that Narendra Modi carries his humility up his sleeves. He maintains a frugal lifestyle free from any indulgences, still remaining accessible to grassroots people and ensuring putting high value on issues of probity and simplicity.

Even in his working style Modi has demonstrated and air for humility by often challenging set norms and precedence. Many who know his working style state that as Chief Minister and now as Prime Minister, he often creates direct platforms of engagement with secretaries and other bureaucrats, many of whom may belong to junior levels in hierarchy, to know about challenges or issues which they might be facing. He would often engage with his junior colleagues in order to provide them with mentorship and support that might be required for them to operate. In the Indian governance system, which lays a lot of emphasis on chain of commands and hierarchy, Modi prefers to operate on open door policy: a trait which indeed emphasises the humility that he carries as a person and respect for the post that he is managing.

Footsteps - Atal Behari Vajpayee

Of all the virtues important for successful leadership, humility is among the hardest to inculcate. It asks one to acknowledge their imperfections and glean knowledge as well as appreciate it, from other people. Among the most popular and loved Prime Ministers in India, Shri Atal Behari Vajpayee is an exemplary example of being humble. He was born in a family of a school teacher in Gwalior and began his career as a poet and journalist before rising to become one of the most widely regarded political leaders of the country. Years later, even during his shining years as a politician and Prime Minister, Vajpayee always displayed graciousness for his visiting relatives as well as everyone else around him.

Al Gore, a prominent American politician and 45th Vice President, in a speech delivered in USA spoke about Vajpayee among an audience of diplomats: "In today's world, it is rare to find a leader who combines the qualities of idealism and pragmatism, confidence and humility. In you, Mr. Prime Minister, we find such a leader." Vajpayee's inherent quality of humility is acknowledged throughout the world. In India, he has been a prominent leader, implemented hundreds of developmental projects and still always stayed away from arrogance.

He is also a man of simplicity. Sometime in 2005, he was gifted a BMW car by the Government of India when it was known that his humble Ambassador car broke down. Narendra Modi reflects some amount of Vajpayee's humility in his public life, taking inspiration from the former Prime Minister. Apart from the fact that both had humble beginnings during childhood and early life, their focus on inclusive politics also echoes their ideals about bringing good to maximum people. Modi promised to continue and carry forward the development policies of Vajpayee in many areas including Bihar.

Though considering Modi's authoritative nature and sharp use of sarcasm, it is slightly difficult to imagine him being gracious to his opponents, as Vajpayee was. Even then, Narendra Modi, backed with an understanding of people and importance of public relations, is most likely to incorporate and apply this quality more than what he already has.

4| Inclusion

"An individual has not started living until he can rise above the narrow confines of his individualistic concerns to the broader concerns of all humanity."
~ Martin Luther King, Jr.

The best and the most effective leaders usually have at the backbone of their authority, a broad inclusive approach. Inclusion means involving, and taking care of everyone in the path to development, making policies that benefit not just the privileged but every other class as well. It includes creating an environment where everyone has the opportunity to fully participate in creating success and where everyone is valued for their distinctive skills, experiences and ideas. Leaders in all kinds of organizations practice inclusion in order to have a balanced, comfortable and motivated workforce. Such leaders are open to opinions, embrace diversity at every stage and understand the importance of development at the root level. At a basic level, management also involves inclusion, where inputs from all levels of operation are taken into consideration for making a decision or implementing an idea. Employee involvement and integrating diversity in organizational processes forms a part of inclusion. It is something that is morally imperative and serves as an excellent business model.

The essence of this concept lies in enabling people to achieve self-sufficiency, something that is quite undervalued and even misconstrued. A leader might sometimes be hesitant in distributing responsibility or authority, but as it derives from the acceptance of one's limitations, an effective leader would practice inclusion in the best manner. Such a practice has a profound effect on empowering people and allowing them to feel like a contributor to overall process of development.

Narendra Modi has been a proponent for inclusive developmental politics, making it one of the key areas of focus in his vision of a developed India. Our country, being a multicultural society has tremendous scope for upliftment and to serve the purpose, leaders need to strive for full participation and equality of citizens. Modi, by developing a vision of inclusion, has set the first step in the desired direction. Sameer Kochhar in his book *Modinomics,* tries to identify the inclusive growth model.

He writes, "Among other things, it clearly articulates that creation of absorptive capacity, economic enablement and empowerment through participatory democracy rest on three pillars of inclusive growth and inclusive economics, namely, social inclusion, digital inclusion and financial inclusion." Modi's vision of achieving inclusive growth involves all three.

Inherently, inclusive growth brings equitable opportunities for the people of a country, making them contributors to economic growth and letting them reap the benefits that are incurred. As has also been demonstrated by East Asian countries, in order to make economic growth work, growth needs to be inclusive. That means making citizens equipped with the necessary skills and proper education so they can be productive.

Until Modi came to power, inclusion in India was understood more from the perspective of region, caste, creed, religion, etc. Sensing that these criteria indeed maintained a status quo of a divided India, Modi's agenda of inclusion in many ways is truly national in its approach and flavour. Since the past sixty years, the adopted methodology of inclusion indeed did more harm than good by excluding people rather than including them. Part of it could be blamed on the personal objectives of the regimes and the leaders and part of it could be blamed on the lack of economic connect. By ignoring the economic connect, Indian democracy thus bifurcated and marginalised some sections while benefiting only a part of the overall population; however, Modi through his policies both as Chief Minister of Gujarat and now as a Prime Minister of India, has undertaken initiatives to include all strata of society.

Going beyond the obvious he has reached out to children (who have often been ignored as a governance constituent), people from the North East, people from different demographic and economic backgrounds, and stating forward an agenda for economic growth. While many would challenge Modi as an inclusive leader, his policies and their implementation have benefitted people from different castes and creeds at large.

His desire for inclusion was evident even during his election strategy where he reached out to ex-servicemen, farmers, businessmen, women and youth individually and in masses to pose his faith in them. If one analyses his speeches and his messages closely, he has always projected himself as a team player and urging various classes to support him in what actually is a cumulative dream of growth and development, with him being just a part on the overall framework of growth.

In his economic vision for the country, Modi has stressed on the importance of development of education, provision of health facilities, construction of an efficient railway and road network, etc. He's also supportive of focusing on manufacturing and services sector to work around the mismatch between imports and exports. His view on e-governance being the most effective form of governance is another indicator of his openness to technology and the confidence in this form of governance as playing an important role in inclusive development.

Modi recognizes the need to reach out to all groups of people and work towards the welfare of all. In his speech in the Lok Sabha in May 2014, Modi talked about the relevance of all sections of society being empowered. He aspires to have the concept of 'development' tapping into a mass movement, so that the goal of growth is something every citizen of the country can relate to. To begin with, this is reflected in the empowerment of ministers under the cabinet and more authority given to the state. Modi also strives to make India's financial sector inclusive in the country's development and to give importance to human resource development, for he believes in the power of young Indians with untapped and till now, underdeveloped potential. India's deficient resources in skills and functionality need to be brought into focus, because employment opportunities without skilled people to make use of them would be a deplorable picture.

Modi's economic vision makes a lot of sense; India

needs good infrastructure, including roads, power, ports, railways and a broadband network. There's a need for easy accessibility of amenities, technological developments and innovation. Although this concept in the government is not new, Modi brings it with clear goals and timelines, and a strong sense of purpose, determination and will to make it happen. Where people are involved, it is always better to lead clearly: having a clear vision, laying out plans for implementation and letting followers know what their responsibilities are and how it'll be constructive. Aimless individuals, groups and societies tend to put the blame on the official authorities and the government, because they are not aware of their own duties.

Narendra Modi also believes in bringing true secularism, where each citizen thinks for the benefit of all Indians and not just a community. He has time and again, reaffirmed his basic tenet that for India's progression, there should be 'justice for all and appeasement to none.' Modi opines that Indians should revert to the original definition of secularism, where for every citizen the primary identity is their nationality. He has always been an advocate for '*sab ka haath, sab ka vikas*' (everyone should be a part of development), stating that his constitutional duty is to serve the needs of all people. Often Narendra Modi has been criticised for working in a manner which is disadvantageous to Muslims; however, if one delves deeper into the data on ground, than it is aptly revealed that Muslims in Gujarat have benefitted equally as have followers of other religions.

A report compiled by National Sample Survey in 2013 led by Amitabh Kundu which analysed state of Muslims post acceptance of Sachar Report in 2006 found that in the period from 2004-05 to 2011-12 the people below poverty line in the state of Gujarat fell from 31% to 7% in rural areas and those in urban areas fell from 42% to 14.6% . Meanwhile, on maximum per capita expenditure, the growth was 39% and 27% respectively. Unlike other criteria, Modi's policy of inclusion is more or less neutral to factors like demography and economic status of the people; rather they have a homogenous approach which in end benefits all.

Taking the example of the state of Gujarat and its economic development, it can be seen how the Gujarat government has pursued an inclusive developmental agenda, not singling out any particular caste, religion or community. Minorities in Gujarat fare as well as the majority community, it being stated that during the "Modi period", the growth in wages of the poor was more than the growth in wages of the richer population. The *panchayats* were empowered and acted as Common Services Centres (CSCs) working towards creation of employment and entrepreneurship. Narendra Modi is being looked upon as a leader who has potential to act and bring about empowerment of people resulting in financial, social and digital inclusion.

While addressing the nation on August 15, 2014, Modi mentioned his 'Digital India' campaign, which he has introduced to encourage Indians to make the best use of technology without any discrimination, making it available for everyone to learn from. One of their main agendas is to empower women by making them come online, which will be facilitated by making it easily accessible as well as user-friendly. To ensure that Digital India succeeds in transforming the usage of digital infrastructure, government services would also be available to the citizens electronically.

Since almost 1.1 billion people are not proficient in English, Google India, that has partnered with the government to help accelerate their agenda for Digital India, has launched nine open source fonts in Hindi and will introduce the same in other Indian languages as well. By way of such measures, Modi is trying to make India an empowered society and a knowledge economy, where technology is central to the change.

As Prime Minister, Modi has also launched the Pradhan Mantri Jan Dhan Yojana (PMJDY) on August 28, 2014, aimed eradicating financial untouchability by opening at least one bank account for every family in a period of six months from implementation. To ensure that families with low income are able to afford a bank account, the scheme has an option for opening a bank account with zero balance. On the inauguration day, over 1.5 crore bank accounts were opened and the Prime Minister said, 'Let us celebrate today as the day of financial freedom.' With its inclusion aspect, this scheme of financial inclusion aims at benefitting all without discrimination and to provide banking facilities and services including insurance and debit, to all. This would also help the poor to get away from the clutches of ruthless money-lenders. The provision of financial access to a wider section of Indians has been seen as an important step in India's social and economic development, as it would inevitably be a positive development for investors and financial institutions as well.

As another example, Modi has also planned to develop villages, for which he has asked all MPs to develop a model village in their constituencies by 2016. This is under the Sansad Adarsh Gram Yojana, where surrounding villages would gradually be built, and take help from, the model villages near their area.

Modi has shown tremendous focus and a strong commitment to this drive, because of which affordable financial services like banking, credit, insurance, investment, pension and financial literacy would be within the reach of a vast population.

An important point worth deliberating is how is

Modi's inclusion is different from the previous regime, which also claimed to be inclusive, thinking about the poor and went into a spree of normally understood social welfare models of MNERGA, cheap food and subsidy based models. Unlike the previous regimes, Modi's model targets where it matters most, which is the economic upliftment of individuals and families through an individual's hard work and systems' simplification. Modi's inclusive model, unlike the one propagated for most times since our independence, is not a typical Big Mamma approach; rather it aims at providing opportunity to all so that the benefits could be enjoyed by all. This model has some inherent benefits as it doesn't categorise a beneficiary based on some demographic or social class, rather it opens up an era of opportunity for all. A factory in vicinity or uninterrupted electricity or reduction in red tapes will provide jobs and economic benefits to all as this is systems driven and not individual controlled.

Modi has also shown his inclusive traits by keeping an ear on the ground and including talented individuals as his team mates. While many would state his approach to be that of Big Brother Watching, yet Modi propagates an internal competition among his colleagues to perform better and show their mettle.

His call of Minimum Government, Maximum Governance echoes his desire for greater inclusion where gradually over past sixty years India transcended from a democracy in nature to socialistic in demeanour. It has now proven beyond doubt that skewed government intervention has indeed resulted in concentration of power and opportunities in hands of few and excluded the common masses of opportunities and governance benefits.

In a country like India where hierarchy and power centres matters the most and political leadership spends a considerable time in maintaining that, Modi shows little preference for them in issues of inclusion. He could have very well chosen to dump his NDA partners post his resounding win in general elections, yet he chose to keep the flock intact. Similarly, by convening a direct meeting with and passing on instructions directly to Secretary-level officers in Indian bureaucracy, he has accorded them an open channel of communication which had not existed till then. While many would view this as surpassing the set norms, many secretaries have welcomed this, as often they are faced with the dilemma of decisions on important matters and thus many a times are also excluded from the policy making process or erratically removed from it. Many of them feel that this indeed is landmark and inclusive in many a sense.

While many would challenge his policies as non-inclusive and polarising, yet Modi's policy and vision (most of which is economic) is clearly inclusive for all and benefiting people of all castes, creed and religion.

This is an important earning for corporate leaders to imbibe that the inclusion of all stakeholders plays an important role in growth of not just an organisation but also of all stakeholders and individuals.

An important differential that Modi has displayed in his quest for inclusion is that he does not shun away from taking responsibility and expects his colleagues to be accessible to general masses. Anyone from India who has had faced some sort of government dealings knows that the biggest challenge for Indian democracy has been its access to masses. Despite a large bureaucracy and governance system, a common man didn't have access to the government officials and leaders at large who would remain in their own citadels surrounded by their coteries. The access to governance was indeed limited to people in power or those who knew the people in power. Understanding this to be a limitation in his inclusion driven agenda, Narendra Modi has ensured that government officials and his ministerial colleagues remain accessible to common masses by working longer hours as well as by providing a transparent form of government. Narendra Modi himself has set an example of accessibility by using both technology and other media to remain connected with people. He has displayed a unique characteristic of synonymising transparency with inclusion which indeed has been missing from the Indian governance system.

Footsteps - Napoleon Bonaparte

Inclusion as a concept has been successfully adopted by global leaders as well, and brought about immense improvement in places where it has been implemented. One such example is The Napoleonic Code in France, named after its propagator and French Emperor Napoleon Bonaparte. It was established in the year 1804 in the aftermath of the brutal and violent French Revolution. This revolutionary code was the first modern legal code to be adopted with a pan-European scope, guaranteeing citizens the right to practice any religion in a predominantly Catholic country (France). It has immense historical significance since it came at a time when the previous government collapsed because of their policies of selective appeasement. This Code emphasized that government policies should be shaped in order to benefit all citizens of the French Empire rather than a particular community. It was successfully implemented and was also very influential on developing countries outside of Europe that were attempting to modernize their country by way of legal reforms, especially the Middle East.

Much like Modi, Napoleon came from a humble background and thus understood that in order to maintain the rule of law and creating congeniality of governance, it is important that systematic interventions are put in place for governing his state. As a leader, Napoleon Bonaparte displayed a unique characteristic of mixing intuitiveness with systems-oriented approach. Narendra Modi has utilised similar systems and intuitive-based models to have a strong grip on affairs of governance and bringing about a creative and intuitive approach for implementation. Many historians have attributed grand success of Napoleon to the fact that he placed his colleagues (including his soldiers and horses) much before himself and took due care of important aspects of warfare logistics and internal governance mechanism of his kingdom, which at one point of time spread from shores of Spain to the mountains of Norway.

Napoleon took the reins of France after the French Revolution, which was an era of chaos for France. In the same way, Modi has taken reign during a time when India faced a slew of governance challenges with corruption and nepotism marring the Indian democracy. Much like Napoleon, Modi has used media as an effective tool to engage with a larger audience. Napoleon brought private media vehicles to France, which emerged as an effective tool for people engagement, while Modi rediscovered the common engagement platforms through novel ideas like *Chai Par Charcha,* Doordarshan Broadcasts or *Mann Ki Baat* programs through All India Radio. While public relations by the regimes are common features, Modi has indeed taken them to the next level by using that as an effective tool for communicating his policies and programs. This is something that has remained absent for decades in Indian polity.

Modi's theme of inclusion closely resembles this Napoleonic Code. India has always been a secular country, but there's need for equitable distribution, which needs to be considered in the new developmental policies. Bonaparte is credited to have instituted lasting reforms including higher education, a tax code, road systems, and with the Code Civil – also called Napoleonic Code - brought about a fundamental change in the civil law legal system. The Code is relevant even in the modern day, its importance ringing in a quarter of the world's jurisdictions such as America, Africa and Europe. Narendra Modi's plans for India seemingly reflect some of Napoleon's ideas.

Even in his personality, Napoleon was known to have a hypnotic impact on people, harbour a photographic memory and be an innovator in his ideas involving financial, bureaucratic and diplomatic resources of France. He could organize teams, make quick plans and implement them to fruition. Narendra Modi as the leader with the immense responsibility of taking care of the country displays similar characteristics. His ideas of distributing quality to all and taking care of each section might seem like an improbable task, but he's set on achieving the feat.

5 | Trust

"The glue that holds all relationships together, including the relationship between the leader and the led is trust, and trust is based on integrity."
~Brian Tracy

Successful leaders share some universal qualities, including having a vision to move a company forward, the foresight to implement ideas and the ability to inspire trust. Trust is perhaps the most important ingredient required for a leader to achieve the desired end results. Trustworthy leaders garner better output as followers feel confident about their goals and thus work with better productivity, loyalty, innovation and high morale. When people place their trust in their leader, it is with conviction that they further act, that they'd be able to accomplish tasks set before them. They trust the leader to make appropriate decisions, reduce the level of risk and take responsibility.

It takes time to build and generate trust in someone's abilities as a leader. The responsible nature of the position makes people think carefully about selecting an appropriate person for the role of the leader. For that to happen, leaders must exhibit genuine concern for the welfare of the organization, enthusiasm and integrity, commitment to deliver and an ability to accomplish goals. Once people believe in the leader's capabilities, they can be counted on to take on more tasks and risk, because they know they have the support and trust of their leader. In order to build a foundation of trust, leaders need to display a sense of clarity, compassion, character, credibility and competency.

By electing Narendra Modi as the 15th Prime Minister of India, the country's citizens have put their faith in him, arising out of the trust he has managed to garner for himself and his capabilities. He has brought forward his past contribution and ideas that were implemented with success, provided enough examples as evidence of his efforts and demonstrated such enthusiasm that people believe him to be a leader who would help India achieve its development goals. Inspiring trust is a capability deriving out of one's understanding of people, but more out of being clear, competent, accountable and diligent. People are also not willing to recognize someone as their leader unless they trust them ethically and morally as well. This is something that Modi has been criticized for, but he nevertheless maintains his energy and belief in his plans to bring India out of its present state of deprivation.

He has also inspired the trust of other world leaders. For example, the recent talks with China and Japan have led to a formalization of plans where the two countries have agreed to invest billions in India – in infrastructure, power projects, railways – because Modi was able to make them trust his leadership by way of initiative, ideas, enthusiasm, optimism and confidence.

Trust as a concept is first and foremost, dependent upon the most important part: being a leader who has trust on his own abilities to perform and leading from the front. The trust in one's own ability indeed is the starting point to rub off the effect of trust on the people around him, who then act as modes of transmission for that trust to other people in general. Narendra Modi displays an intrinsic trust in his own abilities to perform, and leads from the front, thus setting standards of performance for others to follow. The trust in his own abilities conveys the trust to people around him, who in turn, follow him.

A true leader, apart from inspiring trust also trusts his fellowmen and followers, believing in their abilities and providing them due credit. The leader would delegate duties and responsibilities to others, realizing that proper functioning requires delegation of work. By asking the Cabinet Ministers to provide a delegation of work to their deputies, Modi took a step towards inspiring government officials who have the ability to work better than their present capacity. Being called an authoritarian by nature, it is indeed a mark of his good leadership qualities that he understands the need to dilute control. One can take the example of Modi's right-hand man, Amit Shah, who enjoys the absolute trust of Modi for his political insights and organizational skills. He was one of the key strategists for BJP's political campaign for the 2014 general elections.

Narendra Modi, in his speeches at youth conferences emphasizes on the role of youth in uplifting India. He displays an increasing sense of confidence in the abilities of the young population. His focus on improving education by introducing vocational courses and other relevant educational programs to improve functionality and job-skills is just an example of his trust in the country's young and capable people. He also displays full trust in his political party as well as immediate and extended teams and in return, garners their trust in his leadership. Modi has been citing Gandhi's concepts of trust and trusteeship, stating that the government should act as a trustee of the people and in return, trust the people as well. Speaking at one of the investor conferences in New Delhi, Modi said that the challenge for India is not just fiscal deficit, but rather several deficits such as governance deficit, moral deficit, trust deficit, business and security deficit. Talking of it as everyone's responsibility, he said, "If we are able to create an environment of trust, India can race ahead of other countries."

As Prime Minister, Modi strongly pitched for promoting young talent in the Defence Research and Development Organization (DRDO) by ordering five laboratories for scientists under the age of 35. Since DRDO is infamous for working late, Modi tried to show his confidence in them and in the talent possessed by India by ensuring that scientists would be provided the necessary equipment for research, but they'd have to attract young talent. He also advised them to interact with people at the ground level, those who are directly affected by their inventions and innovation, so as to gather better ideas. For the same, hc is considering attaching DRDO scientists to universities, so that they can directly interact with the youth and inspire them as well as generate new ideas. Calling it a 'risk', he stated that he is willing to take it, to give a chance to the youngsters to handle big projects and make big decisions. His faith in human resources such as these often acts as a motivator for people to perform. It hasn't been a very rosy picture, however. Since DRDO has been called 'tardy' quite often, Modi also warned the organization to shape-up in the face of competition from private organizations. To ensure the same, Modi also put the defence minister in charge of conducting a detailed review of the organization. Leaders need to motivate their people, but they also need to ensure that their efforts are not being wasted.

Modi also hailed the Global Citizen movement in New York, USA in September, 2014 when was visiting the country for the General Assembly summit. In this effort to connect with Indian Americans, Modi addressed the enthused crowd with his motivational words that truly showcased his belief and trust in the youth. He said, "Some believe that the world changes with the wisdom of the old. I think that the idealism, innovation, energy and 'can do' attitude of the youth is even more powerful."

Modi's call of "Made in India" reposes his trust in Indian businesses, many of which are struggling due to the Chinese onslaught and opening-up sectors like Defence. This has enshrined his trust in the Indian mind and its capabilities. Since the past decade, India has witnessed stunted economic growth partly due to the global economic scenario and in majority due to the existing policy paralysis which gripped the Indian business climate. Several studies have pointed towards scepticism of Indian businessmen in investing within India, and thus the economic and business trust factor on eve of Modi's ascend to power was the lowest among the business. Sensing this to be a key deterrent in overall growth of India, Narendra Modi ushered several policy level reforms , major ones being in the contentious area of labour reforms to boost not just the productivity of the system but also easing off the labour management system and reporting. Understanding that manufacturing plays an important role in a highly populous country like India, Narendra Modi has been laying an overt emphasis on the manufacturing industries. While till date any reform in labour sector has been viewed with suspicion by various stakeholders, Narendra Modi has been successful enough to ward off that challenge with his creative handling of the situation and urging businesses to not view labour as a challenger or the person on the other side of the table, but working collaboratively towards a single agenda of economic prosperity. Modi thus aims at creating a mutual trust factor among stakeholders so that they would collaboratively work towards a single goal.

He further reiterates his commitment of ensuring removal of bottlenecks and acting as a catalyst to maintain this trust. In one of his speeches titled Shramave Jayate, he reiterated on the commitment of government to increment and improvise on basic technical education at grassroots level so that not only businesses have readily available workforce, but also the working class could improve upon their skills for better opportunities, thus catering to a large and contentious gap that currently impacts Indian economic growth. Like a true leader, he has been using existing challenges as opportunities to convey his larger agenda of economic growth.

His approach is similar to what Alexander used while attacking Darius III of Persia. Darius had an army of million plus while Alexander had an army of a few thousand warriors; however, he knew that Darius's Army was slow as they didn't have the then modern tools like fast horses and agile bows and arrows. Alexander addressed the challenge of a big army by using his military skills of agile logistics to defeat what was then one of the biggest known armies of the western world.

Trust is not developed or inspired overnight. It took years of doing all sorts of work at RSS as a youngster for Modi to get noticed and trusted with bigger roles. It involved proving his abilities by bringing out results and being consistent and loyal. After years of hard work and visible results, he was able to confidently project himself as the right candidate for the coveted seat of Prime Minister of the country. People of one of the largest democracies in the world reposed their trust and confidence in him. Leaders need to recognize the importance of being trusted, of leading by example and assuring their followers that they're indeed on the right path. Without this sense of trust, one's tenure as a leader is fairly limited.

Often people in power thread the fine line of

trust and separating it from nepotistic traits. History is filled with examples of people falling prey to coterie around them which many in political paradigm is misunderstood as trust. However, Modi has maintained a clear understanding and differentiation of the two. His choice of cabinet colleagues or people around him displays a unique ability - giving high credits to performance based trustworthiness. Unlike many leaders in the past, Narendra Modi's trust is not based on just the person himself but his ability and delivery. Winning his trustworthiness has a strong delivery and output component. To put it simply, he follows a simple model of "You perform and you gain my trust." Another important criteria used by him appears to be consistency of delivery. Any management guru will tell you that if there is one word which could replace 'quality' then it is 'consistency'. To achieve the desired results consistently, leaders need to engage with their people and create a process by which the people can achieve better. When one is trusted by the leader, one has a sense of security and a motivation to perform. Trust is a mutual phenomenon.

All those who have been attributed to enjoy his trustworthiness including BJP president Amit Shah, incumbent Haryan Chief Minister, M.L. Khatter , etc have been there due to their personal acumen and delivery and not purely due to any regional or organisational affiliation. Even in his PMO, which since late seventies had become a hot bed for internal intrigues and favouritism, Modi has vested his trust on performers rather than influential people, many of whom are junior officials working in previous regimes, but having a high degree of integrity and dedication for performance.

Footsteps - Nelson Mandela

For any major change to be instituted globally, it takes effective leadership with the leader carrying the trust of his people placed with utmost faith. Nelson Mandela, renowned revolutionary for South Africa's anti-apartheid movement is one example of a trustworthy leader who devoted his life in the pursuit of freedom for millions of South Africans. His trustworthiness is quite apparent in his courage and relentlessness to do the right thing. Even when Mandela was in prison for a period of 27 years, his followers from the African National Congress, where he had later served as the President from 1991-1997, continued to entrust their faith in him and pledged their devotion to him. He was recognized for his strong, reliable and trustworthy character that was reflected in the way he steered forward his strategic agendas.

Narendra Modi with his well laid out agendas for implementation of plans has also come across as being trustworthy with important tasks. Having displayed evidence of his capabilities, he has garnered support and faith in his leadership abilities. Parallels can also be drawn from these leaders' personal lives that reflect their character development into trustworthy individuals. Mandela was known to be a stubborn person, but also loyal and at times exhibiting a quick temper. Typically, he was welcoming and friendly, appearing relaxed in his conversations with everyone, including those with his opponents. Reflections of these traits are observable in Narendra Modi. Along similar lines, Mandela was also said to be image-conscious and sought fine quality clothes, carrying himself in a very regal manner. Modi's favour for good quality *kurtas* especially tailored by his favourite *darzi* is a comparable example.

Above all, Nelson Mandela was a man of principle. Even up against government intimidation, forced imprisonment, and institutionalized discrimination, his supporters could always count on his steady will to pursue their cause. Prime Minister Narendra Modi, in his pursuit of development of the country, needs to be as relentless for the citizens to trust him completely to bring about the desired change.

6| Creativity

"Curiosity about life in all of its aspects, I think, is still the secret of great creative people"
~ Leo Burnett

Most of what we use today is the result of a creative idea. At the heart of innovation lies creativity. Everything new and valuable is born out of unique perspectives of looking at things, situations and people. "Be different" is a slogan much followed by the enthusiastic youth, but most of us miss the real picture. Creativity is simplicity at its best. The most simple, logical and practical solutions for our basic needs is tagged as a creative solution, whereas it is simply going back to base and rethinking, looking at probable solutions from an elementary perspective. One could argue that this is not usually the case, and it might as well be true, but the seed of creativity lies in a balance of imagination and perceived usefulness.

The world is constantly being innovated with new concepts, ideas and technology and all this is based on finding new solutions for the same problems. It is sometimes regarded as a quality only few possess, but inherently, it's possible for all to be able to think of creative ideas. The problem lies in the attitude and perspective. So many individuals never allow their mind to travel out of their comfort zone and thus remain stuck like a well-dwelling frog. People, and most of all leaders, need to realize that they must be able to do away with ages-old ideas that serve little purpose and think creatively. They must become creative problem solvers to deal with problems more effectively.

Narendra Modi understands creativity and evidently has focused on utilizing it along with creating and maintaining a culture that nurtures creative ideas and innovation. Leaders know in their hearts that creativity and innovation are the lifeblood of an organization, the essential tools to be able to sustain a brand. New ideas can lead to such programs that are superior to others. His campaign for the Indian General Elections 2014 can be taken as an example. In Modi's own words, *"When I look back at the entire campaign, three words come to my mind – Extensive, Innovative and Satisfying."* With the unprecedented victory, even his critics are bound to agree that the campaign was indeed creative. The 3-D rallies, *chai pe charchas* and the extensive use of social media made this campaign a success story that generations of politicians are going to study in the hopes to emulate.

However, communication wasn't the only creative part. His policies and style of governance in Gujarat were a stroke of genius that brought Gujarat to the forefront of the India success story. Narendra Modi isn't just creative on his own but he believes in fostering and nurturing creativity at all levels of government. In 2011, Gujarat government launched a scheme to modernize its cities. The planned outlay was INR 7000 crore. The municipal bodies were promised development grants if they were able to establish the right size of administration with an appropriate balance of engineers, planners, administrative staff etc. Since the time-frame was short, the municipal bodies came up with creative ideas to fill the vacancies. They recruited from engineering, architecture and design colleges across Gujarat and offered internships and traineeships. This was a break from the usual bureaucratic process and gave the citizens a chance to be a part of the governance and make a real life impact.

UNIC has even awarded a United Nations award for innovation to Gujarat's government. They stated, *"An innovative scheme designed by the Chief Minister's Office, Government of Gujarat, has been chosen to receive a United Nations award for creativity and innovation in improving delivery, transparency, accountability and responsiveness in public service. The state-wide attention on grievances through the application of technology is an open, transparent system facilitating direct access by citizens, including meeting with their Chief Minister and Senior Administrative Officers. The Senior Administrative Officers are then held accountable for appropriate responses to citizens' grievances'."*

Leaders like Modi search continually for ideas and programs that are better than the present ones and serve the purpose in the most elementary manner. Ever since he took over the coveted post of the Prime Minister of India, Modi has come up with ideas to implement his missions. On August 15, 2014, Modi delivered a speech on Independence Day, where he mentioned a new initiative called the "Make in India" programme. A few weeks later, on September 25, the much-anticipated programme was launched to a great reception. It is a first of its kind initiative aimed at transforming India into a global manufacturing powerhouse by way of getting investors, both local and foreign, to invest in India. Norms, policies and procedures for prospective investors were created in order to make investment in India more attractive. With impressive foresight, Modi is trying to bring out the talent in our country and make it visible around the globe. By identifying local leaders in innovation and technology, Modi would try to make them into global leaders, empowering and encouraging them in the process.

To make this initiative smooth and effective, Modi

has set up systems. He has ensured guidance for investors at every step of the process by way of a separate unit of the Commerce Ministry called 'Invest India'; a dedicated cell and web portal to answer queries within 72 hours; easier regulations to attract investments in infrastructure, facilitating the 100 smart cities project, another creative and innovative venture proposed by Modi. The Make in India program also has further initiatives to foster innovation, protect intellectual property rights and creating better infrastructure as well as promoting state-of-the-art technology.

Many would attribute creativity as something which defies the obvious and in many ways, out of the world, which might not be always true. The "Out of Box" vision often ignores an important component of "Creativity Connect" with stakeholders. Gandhi caught the public imagination with a simple product like salt during his Dandi March. Similarly, Modi caught public's imagination with a ray of hope through his message of "Ache Din" which conveyed a simple yet resonating message of connect. The simple yet subtle message of "Ache Din" could mean different things to different people while having a strong connect to all.

Coming from the grassroots, Modi knew that many a times the technology and development plank in India faces a unique challenge of characterisation. The previous NDA government was scuttled out of power due to

"Shining India", and technology is still considered an urban fiefdom. However, he creatively blended both to give it an approachable look.

Modi's creativity, much like his vision, has a strong flow back mechanism, catching people's imagination with simple yet never thought of systems. Anyone in India could tell the pain that one witnesses during a simple governance process of attestation. While there was no legal reason for it, no one wanted to touch a system which has been existence since the British regime. However, with a simple change of self-attestation (a model followed in best governed systems), Modi not only displayed a sense of creativity in governance, but also conveyed a message of continued creativity, leaving much to think for both his challengers and admirers as to what he will do next.

Modi has used creativity effectively to remain engaged with all stakeholders in general. He does not use it as a one-time concept but rather a continued endeavour. There are very few instances in Human history when creativity is used as a continuous tool of engagement. One could try comparing it with Barack Obama who came on the plank of change and hope but gradually saw the sustenance of creativity diminishing.

Another important aspect of Modi's creativity defies the basic manner in which creativity is understood in normal parlance. Often creativity is attributed to a sudden streak of serendipity and thus its propagators state that it cannot be planned. Modi's model of creativity however has a strong base of planning and vision. He couples his grassroots knowledge and engagement with a fine understanding of simplifying governance entanglement. He presents ideas and systems which on face might sound simple when implemented, but nevertheless appear to people as new and novel. His model of creativity is thus more of re-engineering that absolutely new (of which there is very little chance in India) yet they offer a creative paradigm to masses.

Another example of Modi's creativity is displayed in his approach of connecting with different segments at large and using mediums which had lost out to newer media. His address to school kids across India on Children's day (a segment which has often remained ignored except for ceremonial connect, but holds a great potential as future target) or his addresses through All India Radio (a medium reaching to people who have yet to come in touch with the internet and others) urging the masses to send him ideas indeed has been great success, with PMO receiving 5000-6000 letters daily. These examples are not just simple but rechristen the creativity of governance.

A decade ago when for the first time in India Modi's election campaign used a simple yet novel method of face masks of Modi, India saw another example of simple creativity. In his rallies people would wear simple paper masks having Modi's face and everyone would thus represent a reflection of Modi. His idea caught the fancy of his opponents and compatriots who wilfully followed his creativity and novel method.

While these examples of reaching to masses through simple yet ignored method, Modi introduced the Indian masses to completely high tech methods of 3-D animation. A person in a remote town or village could see a 3D Modi speaking to them and interacting with them; this was not just a technical marvel in itself but a direct connect and a method which was probably used for the first time in the world at such a large scale and with such sustenance.

However, what remains core to Modi's strategy of creativity is his constant desire to remain connected with the masses and electorate which has indeed borne great fruits for him. This is quite unlikely to his peers who generally tend to create a hollow circle around them limiting the access to the common people.

Footsteps - Deng Xiaoping

Leaders across the world incorporate creativity in their plans of action and leadership style in order to make it work. Deng Xiaoping, a Chinese politician and reformist leader of the People's Republic of China, successfully led his country towards becoming a market economy. China was opened to foreign investment, the global market and limited private competition. Xiaoping is generally credited with developing China into one of the fastest growing economies in the world for over 30 years and raising the standard of living of hundreds of millions of Chinese. His creative thinking and innovative policy-making can be seen in Narendra Modi as well.

Unlike his predecessor, Deng Xiaoping knew the importance of economic development. However, he faced the challenge of introducing a diametrically different approach than Mao. While Maoist model was concentration of power and economy of a selected few, Deng's model aimed at decentralisation and using creative methods for growth. Besides his economic and social vision, he, for the first time, broke individuals' power-centre-oriented politics of China and kept the system above individual. He also for the first time was seen more as a people's person by selectively engaging with masses and media, a factor which was completely put on verge during the cultural revolution.

Renowned economist Arvind Subramanian has compared Mr. Modi and Mr. Xiaoping saying, "My Deng Xiaoping analogy is based on three or four reasons. Firstly, Modi represents a decisive break from dynasty rule like Deng Xiaoping broke with the madness of Mao Zedong ideology. Other two things that make me to think further on this are Modi's decisiveness, pragmatic approach and the obsession to get things done like the Chinese reformist leader. Also, what strikes me as a parallel between the two is the kind of long-term horizon for their countries. Of course, the other parallel is that both of them have baggage."

Indeed they have many similarities. There is an excitement around the globe and an expectation that under Mr. Modi's leadership India may achieve success of the magnitude that China did under Mr. Xiaoping. The Chinese economy until the 1970s was majorly agrarian and there was widespread poverty. Its per capita income was even less than India's. However, Mr. Xiaoping realized the potential of China's vast human resources and taking lessons from the economic rise in Singapore, established the concept of Special Economic Zones (SEZs) in Hong Kong. This led to major economic reforms and the policy was replicated throughout China in the next three decades. Mr. Modi too plans on undertaking bold economic reforms to leverage India's vast human resource potential and create an economically developed and progressive India. Much like Deng, Modi's creativity is systematic and result oriented with a clear focus on achievable goals and methods to follow.

As George Bernard Shaw said, *"Imagination is the beginning of creation. You imagine what you desire, you will what you imagine, and at last, you create what you will"*.

7| Optimism

"Optimism is the faith that leads to achievement. Nothing can be done without hope and confidence."
~ Helen Keller

Great leaders can be associated with carrying several traits responsible for their success, but it most certainly cannot be without optimism. In general terms, it means harbouring an attitude of positivity, and an expectation that things will turn out well. Optimism is important because it enables leaders to inspire others by building a compelling vision. As leaders, it is fruitful to emphasize and celebrate the positive results, as well as acknowledge the shortcomings. This gives a very practical, yet bright perspective of the situation and allows people to feel enthusiastic about their work and the organization. Optimism also breeds innovation and hence, creativity. Looking at opportunities in the face of uncertainty and difficulty is one of the best gifts to an optimist. It encourages risk-taking, enables better productivity and elicits enthusiasm. Optimist leaders have an inspiring tone in their communication, which generates a suitable, positive response.

Optimism doesn't necessarily mean staying overly sure of positive results. Logical optimism is what generally works best. Such leaders do not indulge in wishful thinking or strive for unattainable goals arising out of their fantastical desires, but embody qualities that make them look at situations from a broader and more practical perspective. They strive for self-awareness, flexibility, confidence, initiative, adaptability and resilience. These qualities foster their positive attitude that trickles down to the followers and people around them.

Nardendra Modi certainly displays a great sense of optimism, which was also a major reason for his victory in the Indian General Elections 2014. The tidal wave of hope that swept the BJP to power substantiates the fact that optimism is what allowed the party to be what it is and was a major factor influencing their plans, policies and agendas. The government led by Modi has offered a renewed sense of optimism; it is dynamic, robust and has generated an excitement in the people. Modi's attitude of optimism is able to convince that he, and the people, has the ability to achieve levels of performance beyond what was thought possible. He has painted an optimistic and attainable view of the future and substantiated it with his well-planned policies.

A large part of Modi's optimism also comes from his deep understanding and desire to make the change. Narendra Modi has caught people's imagination not purely on the basis of PR or publicity (as many would attribute) but it builds on a solid background of tangible performance which he delivered as the Chief Minister of Gujarat. Sensing that India is passing through a phase of pessimism and governance degeneration, Modi aptly seized on the opportunity of economic optimism. While many would question his style, yet no one would question that Narendra Modi has indeed brought about significant changes in making governance more intuitive and people-oriented. His out-of-the-box idea of covering water canals with solar panels, which not only reduced water loss due to evaporation but also generated solar energy, ensuring 24 hours of electricity supply and making Gujarat a net energy surplus state, etc. not only provided a whiff of optimism to other parts of the country, but was also helpful for him to pass on success to others. His investment events became a benchmark across India and were imbibed by other states of India. The tangibility of sustained results were a necessary act to convey the simple message that indeed his success is not short lived or short term, rather it is a part of a long vision of growth.

An important trait of a successful leader is that they are able to define a clear path of achieving goals, and optimism indeed acts a key catalyst for this. When Christopher Columbus set on the treacherous voyage of discovering an alternate route to India, his crew was sceptical of his venture as they were trying to achieve the unimaginable feat. The optimism of Columbus was ingrained in the fact that he believed that the world was round and if they keep on travelling in the west they will eventually reach the east. This journey led to discovery of newer lands which changed the knowledge of the entire humanity. Reaching out to people and various sections of society, Narendra Modi not only conveys this optimism by imposing trust in his stakeholders, but also elaborating upon the path which might be required to achieve his vision. That way, his sense of optimism appears to be more close to reality and achievable in many ways.

A great leader not only enthrals optimism through his words, but also seeks a message of trust from those who follow him. One of the finest examples of this was displayed when Franklin .D. Roosevelt, spoke as the Presidency was inaugurated in USA, "In every dark hour of our national life, a leadership of frankness and of vigour has met with that understanding and support of the people themselves which is essential to victory. And I am convinced that you will again give that support to leadership in these critical days." Similarly, standing on the pedestal of Red Fort, Modi urged the masses to support him in his objective of a great India, and called himself the *Pradhan Sewak* (Chief/Prime Worker) of the nation rather than a Prime Minister.

Modi is also creative and able to think of innovative solutions, one of the benefits of being optimistic. His plans about development of infrastructure and enhancing investment will have an impact on the economy by improving the willingness of companies and investors to put in new projects. There's hope for different sectors to grow and improve, generate employment and thus affect the standard of living for the better. For successful achievement of his vision, Modi is open to new ideas, willing to see new possibilities, take risks and do all this with confidence. This is a remarkable quality, especially considering his less privileged social and economic background. He doesn't provide his background as a justification of his craving for a public and popular life. Always looking forward, his optimism led him to survive the tedious tasks he was responsible for as a youngster and helped him climb the ladder to a better position.

Optimist leaders find opportunities for development in places where others see none. In our country for example, initiatives to make the rural population technology-friendly are numbered. As Chief Minister of Gujarat, Modi took steps to make this segment of population more efficient and capable by introducing digitization of basic services. What are called 'rurban centres' provide services like digitizing birth and land right record certificates, electricity bills, PDS, etc. This has enabled people to become computer literate and opened up a window of opportunity for them. Now Modi has suggested the creation of 100 new cities with conviction and it can only be hoped that the ambitious project would prosper. There's also an elevated feeling on the matter of low carbon economy. The Indian government in the past, together with the private sector has undertaken efforts to promote a low carbon economy but it is necessary to have an effective set-up for continuous stimulation and monitoring.

Modi, with a strong history of advocating clean energy, has the potential to bring forth a new era of low carbon growth. The rural population of the country lacks access to commercial electricity, which would be taken care of by Modi's vision of utilization of renewable energy and thus unlock opportunities for millions of rural inhabitants. He has publicly supported solar and low carbon, stating that renewable energy is the way forward and has the potential to bring about a desirable 'energy revolution' in India. Even in his speeches, he has always put up an optimistic viewpoint, stressing on his belief that things would work out well for India. When he met the Chinese President Xi Jinping, it was seen as an example of the two countries setting out to strengthen the economic and cultural relations by formally committing to a new beginning that has potential to alter the status quo between the two countries dramatically. Speaking about the occasion, Modi said, "We are now in a different era. We are not living in the 18th century. China is also a country with ancient cultural heritage. Look at how it has focused on economic development; it's hardly the sign of a country that wants to be isolated. That is why we should have trust in China's understanding and have faith that it would accept global laws and will play its role in cooperating and moving forward.

Narendra Modi was present among the hundreds of scientists at the Bangalore command centre of Indian Space Research Organization, applauding the landmark Mars Orbiter Mission, which India achieved in the very first attempt. It was September 24, and India had created history by successfully placing its low-cost Mars spacecraft, Mangalyaan, in orbit around Mars in the very first attempt. "We have dared to reach out into the unknown and have achieved the near-impossible," he said, praising the efforts of Indian scientists and research teams.

Modi has publicly stated quite a few times, in his addresses and speeches to the public and at conferences, that he is quite an optimist. He likes to provide the age-old example of a glass of water half-filled and half-empty, and adds his own, "I say it is half filled with water and half with air" to emphasize on the positive facet of his ideology. Optimist leaders are also surrounded by an air of energy and exude such charisma that it is hard not to trust them and believe in the positive. Modi is a realist as well as an idealist with robust optimism. With his strong government committed to growth, India has a good chance of making it to prosperity since its independence.

What's important here is to note that Narendra Modi is not just viewed as visionary and optimistic person, but as a doer who reposes the faith in stakeholders at large. Improving governance levels has been one of the prime agendas of Narendra Modi, and as Roosevelt stated on the eve of his presidency, "Our greatest primary task is to put people to work. This is no unsolvable problem if we face it wisely and courageously. It can be accomplished in part by direct recruiting by the Government itself, treating the task as we would treat the emergency of a war, but at the same time, through this employment, accomplishing great - greatly needed projects to stimulate and reorganize the use of our great natural resources." Similarly, Narendra Modi has ushered newer investment avenues for the Indian masses and ensured that employment and economic prosperity becomes a central theme to his agenda.

Post his incumbency as Prime Minister of India, the country has been witnessing favourable investment scenarios with Foreign Institutional Investors, Sovereign

Funds and others looking to invest at larger scale in Indian economy. He has also creatively engaged himself with the global geo-political audience at large which has witnessed a renewed faith in Indian diplomatic efforts. During his meeting with Japan and China, two of the largest trading partners of India, Modi has been successful enough to elaborate on economic optimism, which in long run has a rub-off effect on the domestic sense of pride for India.

Footsteps - Barack Obama

The successful and popular leaders of the world are credited to have been infused with optimism and energy that helped facilitate reforms, transformations and bringing about revolutionary changes. Hope inspires and enables not just the leaders, but the people to strive for achievement of their goals. One such example would be Barack Obama, the President of the United States of America, who made history by being the first African-American to hold the office. Obama has been a very positive leader, exhibiting large amounts of optimism and communicating the same to the people by way of his strong speeches and commendable efforts. India is witnessing a similar phenomenon with Narendra Modi, whose vision for the country and confidence in India's abilities has set the wheels in motion. Obama's focus on innovation, investment in research and energy closely resembles Modi's list of goals as well.

Barack Obama came to power when USA was passing through a rather tumultuous phase of economic recession and social chaos. The economic fall recession of 2007 had a rather negative impact on USA's economy, which after the great depression of 1932, saw unemployment and bankruptcy rising. People lost their jobs, houses and many saw their life-long earning turning into junk. Barack Obama came as a renewed hope for common Americans who were depressed and devastated by the corporate corruption and greed. Epitomising the typical American Dream of middle class and as an African American senator, he presented a desire for change. In many ways Barrack Obama and Modi signified rising of people from humble backgrounds who despite their success, were representative of the strata of society that had more or less been devoid of power, and hence their ascent in a way signified a rising force which could improve upon the existing system and create equality and opportunities for all.

Understanding the ethos of democracy and equality, he wrote in his book *Audacity of Hope*, "Another tradition to politics, a tradition (of politics) that stretched from the days of the country's founding to the glory of the civil rights movement, a tradition based on the simple idea that we have a stake in one another, and that what binds us together is greater than what drives us apart, and that if enough people believe in the truth of that proposition and act on it, then we might not solve every problem, but we can get something meaningful done."

In similar ways, Narendra Modi urges various sections of the society to come together to fulfil dream of a much poignant and vibrant India. In his speech titled *Shramave Jayate* (Winning through Hard work), he felicitated alumni of regional Industrial Training Institutes who have risen to great heights, and stated, "Somewhere over the years, the respect given to hard work and diligence has been viewed with scepticism and loss of respect; however, I salute and carry the utmost respect for the people who worked hard to create their own name and it gives me great pleasure to nominate them as ambassadors and representatives of their region, so much so as to giving them preference over political or other leaders."

Obama understands the importance of human resources in the nation and has taken steps to expand education and training, as well as making it more affordable to students. Modi's ideas about improving students' skills in India by introducing vocational training and developing better systems fall along the same lines. These leaders harbour similarities in their public appeal as well: self-confident, charismatic and enthusiastic about their leadership roles. In his Presidential victory speech in the year 2008, Obama had talked about hope and optimism, and how one needs to look at things from a hopeful, yet practical perspective, *"I'm not talking about blind optimism here, the almost wilful ignorance that thinks unemployment will go away if we just don't think about it, or health care crisis will solve itself if we just ignore it. Hope in the face of difficulty, hope in the face of uncertainty, the audacity of hope; in the end, that is God's greatest gift to us, the bedrock of this nation, a belief in things not seen, a belief that there are better days ahead."*

Obama also addresses the youth frequently, believing in the power of nurturing young talent and in his speeches, talks about the importance of having a positive attitude towards any task. Optimism enables one to have a clear vision, determination and energy to accomplish tasks and feel great about it. Modi understands this fact and utilizes it to the maximum, trying to project his optimism to the people.

Both Modi and Obama continuously make it a point to reiterate their vision and optimism for the future and constantly engage with youth, women and different segments of society to maintain the enigmatic component of the optimism and hope. Both are of the view that stating and reiteration of optimism is an important part of overall engagement with their stakeholders. Reiteration of optimistic fervour along with delivery played an important role in re-election of Barack Obama for his second tenure as US President.

8| Adaptability

"It is not the strongest or the most intelligent who will survive but those who can best manage change."
~ Charles Darwin

Adaptability is the ability to adjust to change and learn from experience. The modern world witnesses change at an incredible speed and for a leader to lead effectively, it is important to stay adaptable to those changes. Leaders need to anticipate and respond effectively to change and ensure a smooth transition for their entire team. Great leaders are fearless and can manage change through a clear, strong vision and the ability to adapt to change and enable people to adjust as well.

Adaptability and agility plays an important role in effective leadership. A great leader is the one who is comfortable in all situations no matter what the situation is. While personal adaptability is just one aspect of the overall framework of the domain, a great leader also works towards turning adverse situations into opportunities.

Especially in today's world, where change is the only constant, it becomes critical for a leader to be adaptable to and even appreciative of change. With the complexities of identity, volume of information, rapidity of change and localization of the globe, adaptability has become imperative. Adaptable leaders accept and embrace change. They use emotional intelligence and persuasion to thrive in times of transition. They also act as role models for their teams and help them through change in a productive way. Especially in politics, the onus is high as millions and billions of people are involved. An adaptable leader can set the tone for an entire nation and ensure effective development.

Narendra Modi in his steady assent from tea seller to the Prime Minister's Office, has shown adaptability every step of the way. He has shown a penchant for anticipating, often initiating change to ensure progress. He understands that to lead the way he will have to make change his ally. Rose Fass, CEO of the consulting company Fassforward said, *"The best kind of change comes when you envision, initiate and control it. That type of change creates opportunities, transforms companies and ignites growth. Otherwise, you're facing with the damaging prospect of "change that happens in spite of you, rather than because of you."*

People who have had close working relationship with Narendra Modi vouch that he has a unique knack of adapting himself to any situation or responsibility that is vested in him. Beginning his career as a *swayamsewak,* Narendra Modi rose to the current pedestal by diligently adapting himself with the newer challenges and responsibilities. In 2001 when he was entrusted with the responsibility of taking the mantle of Gujarat he had practically no administrative experience within the framework of government. Considering that Indian governance system is marred with several bottlenecks and with powerful leadership of his predecessors, Narendra Modi quickly adapted himself with the ropes of the game and emerged as an undisputed leader of masses in Gujarat. However, his transition from a secretary in BJP in Delhi to being an undisputed leader was a challenging one with Gujarat recovering from the massive earthquake, as well as BJP facing leadership challenges from its own circles. Modi however smoothly handled the situation through proactive engagement with people from various quarters and adapted himself quickly to the intricacies of the power circle.

A research by U. S. Army Research Institute for the Behavioural and Social Sciences enlisted 8 qualities through which adaptability of a leader could be adjudged:

1. Handling emergencies or crisis situations
2. Handling work stress
3. Solving problems creatively
4. Dealing effectively with unpredictable or changing work situations
5. Learning work tasks, technologies, and procedures
6. Demonstrating interpersonal adaptability
7. Displaying cultural adaptability
8. Demonstrating physically oriented adaptability

Modi qualifies on all these 8 criteria, as well as displays a unique strength of leading by example.

Narendra Modi seems to have a similar philosophy as he preaches as well as practices adaptability. He has demonstrated his affinity for innovative practices and technology as a means to achieve growth and development. He has adopted a pro-active approach for the change management process as can be seen by his massive social media campaign to communicate with the young and aspirational electorate as well as his policies that champion change. He has used Twitter to enhance his connect outside India and he is one amongst the only three who Japanese Prime Minister Shinzo Abe follows on the micro-blogging site.

Narendra Modi has shown adaptability and flexibility throughout his life and demonstrated an ability to transform every adversity into an opportunity. The first campaigner in Hindu rightwing politics to become a chief minister in only thirteen years, he took control of one of India's largest and most developed states even though he had no administrative experience.

Right from his childhood he had shown flexibility and adaptability. He persistently carried out tasks that came his way during his youthful years while working at RSS, performing them with a broad approach. He tried to learn from everything he did and educated himself through practice. He didn't have a knack for formal education, so on the urging of his mentor Lakshmanrao Inamdar, he pursued his BA in Political Science from University of Delhi through distance education. During his reign as the chief minister of Gujarat, he has also drawn policies that used change to further the interests of Gujarat. One such example is of Kutch - one of India's largest salt pan deserts - infamous as a transit point for smuggled goods between the Indo-Pak international border until a few years ago. But in 2006, the global image of Kutch was rebuilt by introducing a 38 day desert festival. Marketed as a cultural extravaganza, tourists from over the globe flock to Kutch to experience its raw beauty and diversity, making Kutch a strong destination on India's tourism map.

Modi deals with a lot of volatility and recognizes the importance of adjusting to unplanned changes as well as changes that shape and move the world. He not only moulds himself into taking out the best of the change, but also keeps a constant watch on any development or issue that has potential for bringing about a change. This keeps him updated and it becomes easy to deal with challenges and make use of opportunities. Leaders need to keep a balance of sticking to their agendas and incorporating the necessary change. Their role involves not just simple change in plans, but also motivating the people to embrace it well.

Footsteps – Deen Dayal Upadhyaya

Deen Dayal Upadhyaya is one of the most eminent Indian philosopher, economist, socialist and historian. He is considered to be one amongst the stalwarts of Bhartiya Jan Sangha and frontrunner of the present Bhartiya Janta Party. Pandit Upadhyaya is also known for conceiving and propagating the political philosophy known as Integral Humanism- synthesis of the material and the spiritual, the individual and the collective. His vision was to have a decentralised polity and a self reliant economy with the village at its base.

Deen Dayal Upadhyaya believed that western ideologies were bearing a negative impact on how India was progressing after Independence. He wanted to seed the original Bhartiya Thought in Indians and wanted them to adapt the modern or western world techniques to their advantage. He considered the ancient Hindu beliefs to be superior to the western theories and asked his followers to be receptive of external influences but not be guided by them blindly. This ideology bears uncanny resemblance to Narendra Modi's style of leadership. He too appears to be at pace with all the modern technologies but the core of all his policies and announcements is his deep love for the ancient theories that drove the Bhartiya vision.

Both Upadhyaya and Modi were born in humble backgrounds and their emergence to such great heights in the Indian political arena is also something worth comparing. Just like Narendra Modi, Pandit Upadhyaya was also known for his sense of humour and a willingness to get his hands dirty in things he took upon.

An adaptable leader is someone who is driven by the attitude of never giving up. Problems and oppositions can come and go, but a leader who continues to strive for the better and keeps surging ahead with a firm footing in his beliefs, is bound to be revered for this courage. Pandit Upadhyaya displayed this attitude at multiple levels. One instance was his firm resolve to voice his opinions through a series of publications that he started. The current mouthpiece of the RSS-*Panchjanya*- was what he started first. When this was banned, he started another and when the second faced a ban too, undeterred, he started a third publication. This determination to get his ideology out to more and more people is so similar to Modi's style of functioning. We have seen him face criticism for a series of measures he has taken up to interact with the public, right from Social Media to *Mann Ki Baat*, but he has not given up on any and used these platforms to let the world know his opinions and visions for this country.

Deen Dayal Upadhyaya viewed both Capitalism and Communism as flawed philosophies. His Integral Humanism was the middle path. He was of the opinion that there should be a 'national sector' where both public-private partnership will ensure self employment and individual entrepreneurship. He wanted economic freedom along with the Right to Work.

He advocated private ownership of means of production but not centralisation of ownership. This vision is visible greatly in the way Modi is stressing on making India a self reliant economy by manufacturing in India. His Make in India campaign encourages Indians to think of newer and fresher sectors where every component of the product or service is made in India.

Modi is also striking a wonderful balance between the western and Indian world by travelling the world, meeting influential leaders of developed economies, learning from them and in turn inspiring his own countrymen to take the positives out of these cultures instead of depending on them for anything.

If we go by the economy where Narendra Modi has successfully implemented this inclusive approach i.e. the rise of Gujarat, we can see that his policies are not in favour of one particular section of the society. He is pragmatic and allows for stakeholders to take their own decisions and choose their own modes of development.

He stresses on fixing the external environment like relaxing the financial policies, formation of ministries who will focus on entrepreneurship and then trust the independent thinking of individuals. Intellectuals say that Deen Dayal Upadhyaya would have largely agreed with this sort of an approach because the basis of all this development is humanism. Laying importance on a Clean Ganga, dreaming of a Swachch Bharat, are all by products of Upadhyaya's theories that development can happen when a leader adapts his/her own thinking as per requirements of circumstances.

Upadhyaya is known to have called the western concepts of world unity, world peace, democracy, socialism and nationalism as good ideals but his belief was they had not been worked well in practice. By investing in these theories and keeping humanity at the core of all this, Modi is doing great service to the ideologies of this great leader.

This streak of adaptability is praiseworthy and definitely an asset of a great leader. He is aware that there is no merit in trashing the modern influences but rather we must use them in our favour to compete with them on equal footing by instilling confidence and positive scenarios.

9 | Communication

The art of communication is the language of leadership.~ James Humes

Clear communication is one of the keys to a leader's success. Leadership in any field is all about having a vision and being able to communicate that vision effectively. Leaders with effective communication have the ability to create substantial positive change and influence people in their personal lives as well.

Politics is only partly about finding the right policies for the time; it is in equal measure about persuading colleagues, supporters and the people that the policies are right. It is about setting a vision before the public and asking them to share it, and by that device to create a bond of common purpose. People generally will accept hardships and sacrifices if they know what the ultimate prize will be, and this requires skilled communication.

History is filled with examples that great leaders indeed have always been great communicators, be it Napoleon who would mount on his horse to motivate his soldiers and countrymen, or Martin Luther King, Franklin Roosevelt and Kennedy. A great leader has an enigmatic impact on the masses that come in contact with him. While many would attribute communication plainly to one's oratory skills, it's important to state that a great communicator is the one who is not just a great orator but also one who is able to articulate and modulate the public feeling and mood and use it towards a position of advantage. The bottom-line of an effective communication is trust and action. An effective leader understands what his audience wants and enshrines a great level of trust in them so that they see him as one of their own. A great leader thus establishes a personal connect with his audience and uses his communication as a tool to reiterate that relationship.

For a political leader his audience could be diverse and heterogeneous, hence it is all the more important for him to address concerns and desires of his audience in a personalised yet harmonious manner. While rhetoric does play its own important role in this domain, what matters most is ingenuity and integrity with which a leader conveys his message to his audience.

In his election campaign, Narendra Modi demonstrated a keen understanding of the importance, the young Indian electorate places on communication and marketing today. And it was this that led BJP to a landslide victory and a decisive mandate- a first in the last 25 years of Indian elections. The man in question was pushed into a superhuman effort of addressing nearly 500 rallies, attending 5200 events and travelling 3 lakh kilometres across 25 states. Added to this was a humungous social media push, and telephonic ads but the combined effort helped the party reach 230 million people across India – an unprecedented figure.

The message was clear: Abki baar Modi Sarkar. People were not voting so much at the level of constituencies or states as they were at the Centre. In the race to victory, Narendra Modi managed to identify the aspiration and ambition of the evolving India and appeal to these very sentiments.

He understood that the youth was united in their shared experiences of history, the availability of information and technology at their fingertips, exposure through media and mobility, and aspirations for education, employment and affluence. And so he chose the economics of development to advance his candidature. He swayed the audience by his impromptu speeches centering on development, diplomacy, investment, infrastructure and national security. He knew that most audiences are less interested in hearing a speech read than in having it delivered in a way that seems fresh and spur-of-the-moment. They prefer dialogue with their elected representative rather than a set speech. He used Google hangouts, twitter, Facebook, televised speeches, TV advertisements, print media, and whatnot to make sure his message got through.

The message and the medium, both were given their due importance and more. Now that Modi has won, his supporters will be quick to point out that he is indeed the greatest of leaders, and the electorate was perceptive enough to know that. But the truth is, Modi and his team knew that the elections are governed by the idea of Out of Sight, Out of Mind. And so strongly visible was the campaign- centered on Modi- that even before the results for the biggest democratic elections in the world were declared, the Prime Minister was elected.

Another important trait that Modi exhibits is a brilliant understanding of symbolism. In a country that thrives on pluralism and variety, symbols can be potent. Modi realizes this; and his attire, body language, gestures and tonality: all are carefully thought out and executed to put across the intended message without scope for ambiguity.

Ralph Waldo Emerson said, "Eloquence is the power to translate a truth into language perfectly intelligible to the person to whom you speak". And Narendra Modi is eloquent. He speaks the rhetoric of responsibility rather than the contented language of entitlements. He comes across as a confident and dominant persona who can catch the crowd's attention. He has created some of his trademark gestures like the V-sign, his hand on his forehead (the thinking man), the clenched fist etc –all signs of being assertive, strong willed and determined.

There is a conscious effort on his part to create a look that connects with everyone. He looks every bit a leader with consideration and reverence for his traditional roots. His aspirational style of dressing- trimmed beard and trademark half-sleeve kurta- have fast become the rage. He carries off his attire well and appears comfortable in his interactions with leaders and followers alike. Modi has leveraged rhetoric, and rustic humour to engage with his audiences. His tone is powerful and grabs the attention.

When Modi went for filing his nomination papers in Varanasi, it quickly turned into a procession: an event he exploited to his advantage. He remapped history and did it proudly, embracing a city that rejoiced in the national attention. He came across as a modernist, a nationalist who sought to blend Hinduism and modernity. This was exactly the image he wanted.

As Prime Minister, he has brought into focus his excellent oratory and communication skills, capable of bringing about excitement and awareness in the masses. Be it openly communicating with the citizens of the country using different technology media for a wider audience, or communicating with other leaders of the world, Modi knows his audience and communicates accordingly. Example, when Modi and Chinese President Xi Jinping addressed the media on Jinping's visit, Modi disclosed to the camera that he had discussed the six-decade old border dispute with the Chinese president, along with the recent intrusions in the Indian territory. Not only does this show his confidence in his actions, it also displays an interest in letting the world know of what is happening. He put his views forward more forcefully as compared to his predecessor, perhaps owing to the majority he holds in the parliament, but more so because he realizes the importance of making his point clear through proper communication. The manner in which he deals and interacts with other leaders sets the stage for a more personalized, and hence powerful, relationship.

Footsteps - Sir Winston Churchill

Narendra Modi's style of communication highly resembles that of Winston Churchill, best remembered as the British prime minister whose speeches rallied a nation under a relentless Nazi onslaught in World War II. Churchill was particularly noted for his speeches and radio broadcasts, which helped inspire the British people. He did not pretend more erudition than he had, a quality reflected in Narendra Modi.

Churchill was globally known for his scathing stand against the Nazi onslaught and for taking his opponents heads-on. In his famous speech, *Blood, Toil, Tears and Sweat,* he stated, "We have before us an ordeal of the most grievous kind. We have before us many, many long months of struggle and of suffering. You ask, what is our policy? I can say: It is to wage war, by sea, land and air, with all our might and with all the strength that God can give us; to wage war against a monstrous tyranny, never surpassed in the dark, lamentable catalogue of human crime. That is our policy. You ask, what is our aim? I can answer in one word: It is victory, victory at all costs, victory in spite of all terror, victory, however long and hard the road may be; for without victory, there is no survival. Let that be realised; no survival for the British Empire, no survival for all that the British Empire has stood for, no survival for the urge and impulse of the ages, that mankind will move forward towards its goal. But I take up my task with buoyancy and hope. I feel sure that our cause will not be suffered to fail among men. At this time I feel entitled to claim the aid of all, and I say, come then, let us go forward together with our united strength."

In similar terms, Narendra Modi's speeches are filled with high octane emotive metaphors yet remaining pertinent with the mood of his audience, who remain enthralled by his oratory tempers. However, it's important to state that much like Churchill, Narendra Modi has a strong understanding of the pulse of his audience and a large body of communication is customized according to the region in which he is giving his speech. This has been a vital differential for Modi and making him a leader who commands national appeal. Coming from a relatively small state with marginal political impact on national politics in terms of members of Parliament that it sends to the national Parliament, communication indeed has been one of the major reasons for the rise of Narendra Modi.

Interestingly, both didn't fit into the standard educational system despite the tremendous talent they possessed. Another parallel is the both of them were resilient and never let their inherent disadvantages hinder their progress. While Mr. Modi is looked down upon for not being fluent in English by the intellectual elite, Winston Churchill too had a speech impediment: something he worked to overcome. Both of them did not let this stand in way of their public speaking and let their actions speak for themselves.

Both Mr. Modi and Mr. Churchill had ambition and intelligence: traits that led to their immense political success. Mr. Churchill wrote in a letter to his mother, "it is a fine game to play- the game of politics- and it is well worth waiting for a good hand before plunging in". Both could see the big picture and favoured market based policies to stimulate demand despite the criticism from socialists. They were eloquent and charismatic and used their personalities in political leadership.

Winston Churchill's style of speech was evocative which is quite similar to that of Mr. Narendra Modi. Who could forget his multiple speeches on the issues of the need for change, factionalism in the Congress (calling Mr. Rahul Gandhi a Sheehzada)? Both began their speeches strongly, used simple yet personal and colorful language to engage audience and drew a picture in the readers' minds through imagery and rhetoric. Also, both ended with an emotion.

Like Narendra Modi's political isolation after Godhra riots, Winston Churchill too faced unpopularity after the Dardanelles expedition. But they were strong and uncompromising even in the toughest of times. Churchill once said that dictators were afraid of the power of words. "A state of society where men may not speak their minds cannot long endure."

10 | Emotional Intelligence

"Emotion has its place, but it must not interfere with taking the appropriate action."
~ Susan Oakey-Baker, Finding Jim

Daniel Goleman, popular psychologist and author of widely-acclaimed books on psychology, science and leadership defines Emotional intelligence (EI) as 'the ability to monitor one's own and other people's emotions, to discriminate between different emotions and label them appropriately, and to use emotional information to guide thinking and behaviour.'

In the modern scenario, most people believe that emotional intelligence (EI) is more important than one's intelligence (IQ) in achieving success in their careers and lives. Today, the success of individuals and the profession depends on the individual's ability to read other people's signals and then react appropriately to them. Especially as the economy has become more global, it has increasingly become important to have Emotional intelligence skills so as to better understand, empathize and negotiate with other people.

Howard Gardner, an influential Harvard theorist states, "Your EQ is the level of your ability to understand other people, what motivates them and how to work cooperatively with them." This understanding of what motivates others, being able to relate to people in a positive manner and to build stronger bonds with others in the workplace makes those with higher emotional intelligence better leaders. An effective leader is one who can recognize the needs of his people, aiming to meet those needs in a way that encourages higher performance and workplace satisfaction. An emotionally savvy and intelligent leader is also able to build stronger teams by strategically utilizing the emotional diversity of their team members to benefit the team as a whole.

Emotionally intelligent people accept and are comfortable talking about their limitations and strengths, often demonstrating a thirst for constructive criticism. This opens them up to their team members and followers, who are able to generate their trust in them. By contrast, people with low self-awareness feel threatened with criticism and interpret it as a sign of failure.

Self-aware people can also be recognized by their self-confidence. They have a firm belief in their capabilities and are less likely to bring about their own failure, for they have the foresight and patience to understand their limits. They are less likely to take up a challenge that they know they would not be able to handle. Leaders who assess themselves honestly would do the same for the people they lead.

Narendra Modi has demonstrated remarkable emotional intelligence in his rise to power. But nothing explains it as his response to the post Godhra riots. In the aftermath of Godhra riots, Narendra Modi faced political and social isolation for years, in what is now termed by many as a premeditated attempt at his political assassination. It wasn't just a nation united in its fury over the killings, Modi even faced flak internationally with the US and UK refusing to grant him Visa for tours. Yet he bore it all with a silent dignity rather than emotional responses. He admitted to sadness on what had happened but not to guilt and submitted himself and his ministers to a special investigation and came out unscathed with the SC exonerating him of all charges levelled against him. Through all this, he managed to be the longest serving Gujarat Chief Minister before rising to be the Prime Minister of India. In handling all the turbulence and bashing, Modi has demonstrated immense emotional intelligence and stability.

An important aspect of an emotionally intelligent person is that he remains focussed on his vision and mission and does not deflect from his objective. Apart from Godhara riots, Modi faced challenges in terms of rehabilitation efforts of Bhuj earthquake and still-to-be-recovered Surat after the massive outbreak of Plague in 1994. However, despite facing all sorts of challenges, Modi motivated and cobbled up an exceptional team of administrators and officials along with ministerial colleagues in converting the salty parches of Kutch into one of the best examples of industrial development and Surat into one of the cleanest cities of India.

While many would attribute that Narendra Modi displays an aggressive stature which sometimes challenges the basic definition of emotional intelligence, his aggression is focussed and cannot be stated as merely an emotional outburst. Rather, it has to its core, a desire to prove his point and that too with a great degree of commitment and vigour.

He has also exhibited intelligence by leading an aggressive campaign appealing to the collective aspiration for a decisive government. And now that he has been brought in as the Prime Minister with a decisive mandate, he has started by forging relationships at work and with the neighbouring countries. Narendra Modi has a high emotional intelligence quotient which he has used effectively in his strategically planned communication. Responding to the paranoia of the leftist elitists and the general mood of the public, he has wisely and categorically stated that life stories of living individuals should not be a part of school text-books. At the same time, he has kept silent on the controversy raked up on Article 370 and allowed it to die a natural death.

He has cleared the air from day one and demonstrated that the focus is on measurable results and outcomes. The channel of Empowered Groups of Ministers and Group of Ministers has been scrapped in tandem with his dictum of "Minimum government, maximum governance". The thrust is on inculcating a culture of efficiency and hence, bureaucrats have been asked to take responsibility commensurate with delegated authority.

Capitalizing on the optimism surrounding the new government, he has seized the opportunity to make announcements on otherwise unpalatable issues such as FDI in defence, structural changes in the MNREGA and Food Security Act. He knows his strength is economics and has used every opportunity to convey that to the public. Another tactical measure he has taken is that of preparing the nation for some tough economic decisions that he will have to take to revive the economy. He realizes that taking up unpopular measures might make him so and he has already softened the impact by making the electorate aware of his stand.

At the same time, he has broadcasted the current

weak state of the Indian economy and asked the people to hold his government accountable from the third year onwards. He has clearly communicated that now he has the requisite authority, he plans to be a statesman and not a politician. His focus appears to be on the seven E's – Education, Entrepreneurship, Employment, Equity, Empowerment, Economy, External Relations and Environment.

Modi uses his intelligence especially when it comes to dealing with different kinds of people. For example, Modi went an extra mile and publicly hosted the Chinese President Xi Jinping in Gujarat and in the process, sought to deliberately inject warmth into talks between India and China, looking at a broader goal. With this effort, he managed to convince China of India's resource capability as well as talent, so that China would commit to invest in the country.

He faced scathing criticism when he invited Pakistani Prime Minister Nawaz Sharif for his swearing in ceremony due the acrimonious relationship between India and Pakistan. However, as a sharp statesman, he understands that issues of disputes could only be resolved through proactive engagements and not otherwise. Even during that visit Narendra Modi ensured that India's stand be put forth in a definitive manner, and it must be ensured that India is committed towards harmony and peace in the region. Separating the geo-political stand from the personal one, Narendra Modi like a skilled statesman, created a personal rapport with the Pakistani premier by gifting a shawl for his mother, which according to the Indian tradition, states a mark of respect for one's elders and thus respecting the tradition and conveying brotherhood and love.

In the same manner, Modi decided to address Indian Americans at Madison Square Garden in New York, to express his gratitude to them. This announcement was met with a lot of fanfare, with the place, usually reserved for musicians and rock bands, being sold out for the first time in history. He used the stage to ask Indian Americans to help develop the Indian economy. In the same visit when he visited Central Park in New York, he began his speech with, 'How are you doing, New York?' These are the little things he does that are sure to ring with his audience at an emotional level and make them sway in his words.

Emotional intelligence is about being sensitive to friend and foe alike, and trying to find common ground, even at times where there is significant disagreement. This is especially a struggle in the political arena where all discussions are highly charged. But an emotionally intelligent leader knows when to diffuse the tension. After his election, he was seen greeting the members of other parties cordially. A political party's own survival is dependent on its ability to stretch itself in this way. A vibrant, engaged party is critical for spirited debate and imaginative, balanced policy.

Contrary to myths, an emotionally intelligent person also displays softer characteristics of love and respect, and there are ample examples of such nature displayed by Narendra Modi. Often he is seen visiting his family and spending quality time with his aged mother, sitting and serving her. He is known to be particularly fond of poetry and finer literary tastes and many people who have had a chance of working along with him find him to be grounded, compassionate, loving and caring. He is known to reach out to people and inquiring about their personal well-being and respecting their emotions. He is blessed with sharp instincts and memory and makes sure that everyone gets personal attention when meeting him.

Footsteps - Ronald Reagan

Nicknamed the great communicator by his contemporaries, Ronald Reagan, the former U.S. president, used his emotional intelligence to convince his constituency and disarm his adversaries. He put a great onus on connecting with people and developing meaningful relationships and this made his leadership an unprecedented success.

There lies great similarity between the political and economic situation that impeded Presidency of Ronald Reagan and that of Narendra Modi. When Reagan took the Oval Office, America was passing through one of its worst economic and political phase. The pursuant triple economic recession that began in early 70s had reached its prime with a double digit unemployment rate, with interest rates hovering close to 25%. For the first time in many years, Americans were witnessing inflation and it was posing to be a real challenge for any incumbent President. The economic trust was at its lowest and the benchmark Dow Jones Index lost almost 70% in the decade preceding ascendancy of Reagan on the top post. Sensing the key challenges, Regan undertook a model which eventually was known as Reaganomics (a joiner for Reagan and Economics). He gradually took massive steps towards deregulation, reducing government expenditure, rationalising taxes and undertaking steps to curtail inflationary pressures by regulating money supply. His steps indeed had an historic impact and America witnessed a spree of growth which remained with it for decades. Despite the economic and political challenges, Reagan kept economic policies to his central theme.

In similar terms, Narendra Modi has come to power in India at a time when the Indian economy is passing through is most challenging times with stunted economic growth, high inflation and economic challenges. Modi's strategy of Less Government and More Governance is reflective of the Reagan model. His emphasis on critical issues of disinvestment, improving investment climate and rationalising of taxes and others bears a close resemblance with the Reagan model as well.

What's important here is that both leaders took the challenge of poor economy heads on and found out distinct and novel ways to handle it. This characteristic thus reflects an extremely high level of emotional quotient which remains unfazed by the challenges it faces and works creatively to resolve it.

Clear parallels could be drawn with Narendra Modi who believes in being a part of the message. He is working on developing mutually beneficial relationships with not only ministers and bureaucrats but also his allies and adversaries abroad. Modi bears striking similarities to the celebrated American president. Both men rose from humble origins. Both were popular and successful state governors before rising to head their countries: Modi was the chief minister of Gujarat and Reagan the Governor of California. Modi, like Reagan, is an unabashed proponent of free market economics: "Modinomics," the term coined to describe Modi's free market and anti-corruption reforms, is of course a nod to "Reaganomics".

Another common denominator between the two men is the nature of their censurers. Both faced cultural elitists who despised them. Reagan was labelled a racist, a term that is used for anyone who believes that a strong and growing market economy, rather than massive government bureaucracy, is the best way to promote upward mobility for the poor and minorities. Modi, a proud Hindu, is also termed a racist by his critics.

Both men exhibited a high degree of emotional intelligence which is evident in their rise to power despite the surrounding criticism. They understood that the sender is a part of the message and used non verbal communication to relate to their electorate powerfully on a personal level. Both had big dreams and ambition that they shared with their teams and audience. They understood that true belief is contagious and that success only comes after a vision and plan.

Modi understands the importance of connecting in a compelling way and uses rhetoric to make them understand the power of his dreams. Reagan too allowed audiences to join in the adventure. He called the Soviet Union the "evil empire" and his listeners understood. He referred to the United States as "the shining city on the hill," and people were inspired. Through common, visual language, he created images and concepts that energized action.

Just like Reagan, Modi is an eternal optimist and understands public aspirations. He suggests that tomorrow should be better than today and today better than yesterday. Reagan understood that strength requires restraint. Mr. Modi too knows how to manage his strengths and weaknesses. He realizes that he cannot micromanage everything. He backs on his team and serves as their tutor, motivator, sponsor and role model. He understands that talented people need the freedom to do things themselves in their own ways lest they lose interest in their work and become mere robots. And just like Reagan, he has created a participatory model of work.

The Reagan era is also marked by the potential rise of the American Enterprise which expanded their global horizons and made many US companies truly multinational. Reagan emphasised the need for American enterprises to think beyond the shores and thus trusted the enterprises to create economic value for the nation and the globe. In the same way, Modi through his "Made in India" call has entrusted a completely indigenous model of strength for India's economy, as well as providing an opportunity for Indian businesses to make greater investments in domestic markets of India, which today is one of the largest in the world on the basis of its sheer size.

Also, even though Reagan called the Soviet Union the evil empire, this did not prevent him from negotiating and dealing openly with the leaders of that empire. Mr. Modi too, despite his strong and negative rhetoric on Pakistan in his election speeches, has proved to be flexible and collaborative in his dealings with Pakistan for the good of India. He has adjusted his views of the enemies and is working to transform them into partners in building peace.

Ronald Reagan said, *"Peace is not the absence of conflict; it is the ability to handle conflict by peaceful means."* Emotional intelligence is a prerequisite to understanding and implementing this philosophy.

11| Leveraging Information and Technology

"This is why I loved technology: if you used it right, it could give you power and privacy."
~Cory Doctorow

Technology has changed the way we live. Our standard of living has increased and we have access to greater comforts which at a time would have been considered luxuries. Advancements in agriculture have led to increased food production; advancements in civil engineering to sky high buildings and robust infrastructure. Technology has boosted every industry. Businesses have grown and so has employment. There is increased research in fields ranging from genetics to extraterrestrial space. The computer and Internet technologies are ubiquitous. They have changed every sector; be it medicine, tourism, education, entertainment or any other.

Technology has also changed the way people communicate. Communication systems have evolved from birds carrying messages to emails and instant messages that traverse the globe in nanoseconds. In this age of information and technology, when every sentence, every word can have an explosive effect, it becomes important for leaders to acquaint themselves with technology and ensure that their messages reach the tech-savvy electorate exactly as intended. Leaders need to leverage technology to create change and a positive one at that. The magnitude of that change will also be impacted by the scale of technology.

Narendra Modi has shown great intuitiveness in the way he has accepted, embraced and even propagated technology as the panacea to all problems. He understands that with technology come efficiency and speed. They save human effort and time to a great extent and make life easy and comfortable.

Narendra Modi has been emphasising on extensive usage of Information Technology in the governance domain. Gujarat has been a pioneering state in the usage of e-Governance and M-Governance. Modi sees Information Technology as a great equaliser and a tool to reach out to the masses.

The BJP and Modi ran a carefully orchestrated tech-savvy campaign of a colossal level that directly engaged voters through social media, amplified his appeal and maximised his reach. There was large-scale usage of technology; open-access internet platforms to connect, build conversations and share opinions. Modi clicked campaign selfies that went viral and even appeared as a holograph at campaign events. A man ahead of his times, he has been active years now on the micro blogging site- Twitter- and has a huge following. He knew that the India that will vote for him comprises a population that lived on internet. And so he chose his weapons: Facebook and Twitter. He used video messages, tweeted in all Indian languages, conducted 3D rallies online and had hashtag wars with competitors. His victory tweet was a testimony to his social media success - 'India has won' was retweeted over 40,000 times within mere minutes.

By the time 2013 Assembly elections concluded, he had eight million fans on Facebook. His fan base crossed fourteen million fans by the end of Lok Sabha elections – making him the second most "liked" politician on Facebook after Obama. Ankhi Das, the public policy director for India and South Asia at Facebook wrote for an article in Quartz, "*Openness, sense of community, and freedom are inherent characteristics of the internet. These attributes both helps build momentum, mobilize and also challenge. Political parties will need to recognize this and embrace this equalizing tool. Those that do will succeed. In politics you will have to connect and share. Ultimately these are core values of a vibrant democracy. The 2014 election results firmly established that."*

And now that the man has won, he plans on using technology to build a stronger and smarter India. Mr. Modi, a firm believer in the power of IT has proposed its disbursement to all sections of society to improve India's global standing. He has advocated IT to minimize corruption and empower the common man. He believes that technology can be used to leverage India's vast human resource capability and make India the hardware and software hub of the world. He has time and again reiterated that technology has become a key role player in delivering good governance in politics. He understands that internet has brought about a paradigm shift in the way the administrators and politicians connect with the citizens and that the crux of politics lies in connecting with the people.

"For me, e-governance is easy, economic and effective governance!" he says.

During the 25th Nasscom leadership summit in Mumbai through a webcast, he said, *"IT has the power to transform the country in several ways. I see IT as a change-agent. It empowers, connects and can bind isolated parts of the nation and create harmony. IT can join people with governments, bridge the gap between demand and supply, and can bring us closer to knowledge. We must bring down the digital divide. We can't have two Indias, one racing ahead and another moving on a reverse gear. This will add to our problems. Just like the British built bridges and rail lines, information highway network can today play a very big role in transforming the nation. I keep saying that IT+IT=IT (Indian Talent + Information Technology = India Tomorrow). The IT sector can be the shining light of Brand India."*

And he doesn't just talk. His home state, Gujarat, where he served as the Chief Minister for over a decade, is already an e-governed state and has initiated several innovative applications. The state is an innovator when it comes to incorporating technology into Governance. Initiatives such as Swagat Online, Tele Fariyad have brought in transparency and given the citizens a chance to interact with the highest office in administration citizens to make themselves heard and to make them feel content and justified. His e-governance initiatives have become widely popular and have received global recognition. Under Gram SWAGAT program, aggrieved citizens in villages can lodge their complaints at the E-Gram centres. These complaints are then taken up by the Taluka Mamlatdar and are solved in a time-bound fashion. Gujarat has also been successful in connecting villages with the largest broadband connectivity called e-Gram Vishwa Gram Yojana.

Now as Prime Minister of India, Modi doesn't hesitate to express about his ideas to the citizens of India, or to the world, and tries adopting various ways to do so. One of the unique ways he adopted for the same was on September 5, 2014. Breaking away the traditional manner of celebrating Teacher's Day in schools, Modi, through a notification issued by the Directorate of Education (DoE) of Delhi government, asked all private and public schools in the county to listen to him talk live with students. For the same, he made use of televisions, set-top box connections, internet, projectors, screens, generators and amplifiers for the large-scale video conference, making those available on a hiring basis in case some schools didn't have them. His address was broadcasted on TV, radio and the internet, making it available for everyone. Although this drew a fair amount of criticism, owing to the fact that the notification made it mandatory for all schools to do so, the success of this path-breaking initiative as Modi light-heartedly, yet inspiringly, addressed students across India, was widely appreciated. Not only did he inspire the students with useful anecdotes and stories, but also addressed important issues such as girl education. As a leader who understands his audience and his power, he also used this platform to encourage the young minds of the country to share their knowledge and help make education better. This initiative could be seen as one laying foundation for building a world class human resource, which would be much in demand as the country opens up its various sectors and requires talent to run them.

In his various addresses, Modi makes full use of his oratory skills as well as available technology, so that each time he comes up to address a gathering, it seems like the whole world is one big classroom, listening intently.

He understands, and makes use of, the power of social media too, as is evident from the fact that his election campaign heavily used the internet to connect with people. Modi is among the top when it comes to Twitter followers and has enabled most of his programs and schemes to have dedicated websites. Among the most popular ones is MyGov (mygov.in), a people-centric website to allow citizens help in good governance by providing their opinions and views on important issues, such as girl child education, Digital India, job creation, etc. They can also get information on various social schemes of the government, as well as take a look at different projects. As part of the Digital India campaign, he has brought together mobile service providers to assist in the project. For example, BSNL is contributing to provide a national optic fibre network (NOFN), Wi-Fi hotspots at commercial places, mobile services under the Jan Dhan Yojna and delivering mobile government services like kisan seva and digital mandi.

As a leader, Modi realized the importance of people's ideas on various issues of national importance, since they are the ones directly affected by it. Creating such opportunities for idea generation by identifying untapped resources is something good leaders indulge in. He understands that in leading a nation of 1.2 billion people, technology will pave the way to progress, growth and development.

Besides all this, Modi has also been at forefront of investments in all kinds of technology, including clean and renewable energy. During his tenure as Chief Minister of Gujarat, Modi was successful in getting close to a $3 billion worth of investment in clean energy. His ambitious Canal Solar Power Project - installing solar panels mover the Narmda River Canal system is estimated to generate 1.6 million units of energy and saving 9 million litres of water annually which otherwise would have been lost due to evaporation .

Modi's technology-oriented approach indeed has been recognised globally. John Kerry, Secretary of State, USA, in his speech after Modi's election as Indian Prime Minister at the Centre for American Progress' India: 2020 Program stated, "And now, it's not hard to see how in this moment, we can actually deliver on that partnership's full promise. The new Indian Government's plan, "*Sabka Saath, Sabka Vikas*" – Together with all, Development for all – that's a concept, a vision that we want to support. We believe it's a great vision, and our private sector is eager to be a catalyst in India's economic revitalization. American companies lead in exactly the key sectors where India wants to grow: in high-end manufacturing, in infrastructure, in healthcare, information technology, all of them vital to sort of leapfrogging stages of development so you can provide faster to more people."

Footsteps - Bill Clinton

"Investment in technology drives economic growth, generates new knowledge, creates new jobs, builds new industries, ensures sustained economic and national security, and improves our quality of life ... My balanced budget plan maintains vital investments in science and technology ... That is the common ground on which American economic progress and quality of life depend."

~President Bill Clinton

Bill Clinton, in his eight year tenure as the President of United States, is credited with having used IT to establish an open and transparent governance model. Executive order 13011 asked heads of central government's agencies to utilize IT as a means to transparency. The top-down approach of the government combined with the bottom-up thrust from businesses had a ripple effect throughout the globe. India's IT revolution began with the huge demand of low-cost IT products in America. In this, he can be compared with Modi who is also a strong proponent of leveraging technology as a means to economic growth and development. But the similarities don't end here.

In his state of the Union Message to the Congress in 1998, Bill Clinton stated, "We should enable all the world's people to explore the far reaches of cyberspace. Think of this: The first time I made a State of the Union speech to you, only a handful of physicists used the World Wide Web - literally, just a handful of people. Now, in schools, in libraries, homes, and businesses, millions and millions of Americans surf the net every day. We must give parents the tools they need to help protect their children from inappropriate material on the internet, but we also must make sure that we protect the exploding global commercial potential of the internet. We can do the kind of things that we need to do and still protect our kids. For one thing, I ask Congress to step up and support for building the next generation internet. It's getting kind of clogged, you know, and the next generation internet will operate at speeds up to 1,000 times faster than today."

Similarly, Modi in his Independence Day Address stated, "Some 25 to 30 years ago, the world used to think we are a land of snake charmers and black magic. But our youth has surprised the world with its IT (Information Technology) skills; I dream of a digital India. It was once said that railways connects India. Today I say IT connects India... I fully believe a digital India can compete with the world."

While Modi is the first Indian Prime Minister to have been born after India gained independence, Clinton too was the first U.S. president born after the 2nd world war. Both have served the state before serving the centre.

A man ahead of his times, Clinton has been credited with implementing policies to enhance spending in research and development to build infrastructure. In his book, Back to Work: Why We Need Smart Government for a Strong Economy, he says, "Our ability to compete in the twenty-first century is dependent on our willingness to invest in infrastructure: we need faster broadband, a state-of-the-art national electrical grid, modernized water and sewer systems, and the best airports, trains, roads, and bridges."

Modi too has listed infrastructure building as one of his ten priorities. Also just like Modi, Clinton too understood the dreams and ambitions of his countrymen. In the 1993 presidential elections, he along with Al Gore- his chosen Vice-Presidential candidate- set out by bus to meet the people of America and to hear about their concerns and their hopes for the future. They campaigned on the concept of 'putting people first' - preserving the American Dream, restoring the hopes of the middle class, and reclaiming the future for the nation's children.

12| Individuality

"Most of us find our own voices only after we've sounded like a lot of other people." ~Neil Gaiman

Acceptance and expression of one's own individuality and personality is critical to leadership. Individuality refers to the set of characteristics that differentiate an individual and set him apart. A person who demonstrates a strong sense of individuality shapes his life on the basis of his own convictions and beliefs without depending on others' approval. Individuality is often positively correlated with creativity, original thinking, scientific discovery and social innovation and encourages one's self-reliance, initiative, persistence and unique perceptions and new visionary ideas.

When an individual has a unique point of view that may not conform to the society's view, it gives way to creative ideas and innovation. For example, Sir Isaac

Newton formulated the law of gravity on observing an apple that fell from the tree. Apples' falling from trees is a pretty common phenomenon but no one before had contemplated over it and had merely accepted it as an everyday occurring. Similarly, Copernicus had a unique view that led him to discover that the earth revolves around the sun and not the other way round. Individuality leads to original thinking and the courage to challenge the established beliefs.

Narendra Modi too demonstrates individuality in appearance and in action as he climbs up the ladder to power, courting controversy and receiving praise and blame alike. From tea-seller to the Prime Minister of the world's biggest democracy, he has shown an inimitable and strong personality and capitalized on his uniqueness. He never backed from an idea that he thought would work regardless of its popularity and pushed through countless reforms and policies that have changed the face of Gujarat and will hopefully better India's global standing now that he is the Prime Minister.

Narendra Modi had nurtured high ambition from childhood itself, something he isn't ashamed to admit. And yet, he does not romanticize with poverty. Despite his humble beginnings, today he has become one of the most charismatic leaders with a personality that brought the most decisive mandate in the Indian elections in almost 30 years. His political mentor Shanker Singh

Vaghela said in an interview to The Hindu, *"From the early days itself, he was always particular about creating a different identity for himself. If they wore khaki shorts in the RSS, he wore white. If others wore a red thread around their wrists, he sported a black one. His shoes too were different. He was always conscious about his whole look and had a passion for photographs."*

It may be a cliché, and you can love him or hate him, but you can't ignore him. One of the fiercest leaders of his age, he has a strong personality with his own set of characteristics, style and charisma. In April 2009, long before Modi ascended the throne, Robert Kaplan wrote in The Atlantic: *I have met Jimmy Carter, Bill Clinton, and both Bushes. At close range, Modi beats them all in charisma.*

Modi's vision and approach reflects a great degree of individuality and concentration of the basic issues which matters to the common man. Bindeshwari Pathak, a globally renowned figure and promoter of the Sulabh Movement, in his recent interview with a news website Fijeeha stated that after Mahatma Gandhi, Narendra Modi is the first person to have picked a broom and speak about basic cleanliness and due to him, cleanliness has indeed become the core focus of leading personalities and corporate, who till date ignored it. His approach thus has the mesmerising impact of connect with people, something which not only displays his priorities, but also individuality of the character.

Modi closely comes across as a brand whose symbolism is all about his personality; a decisive one with such force that it is capable of breaking previous years' incapacity. Standing tall, he has an expansive body language. Hands in front of his chest, he doesn't slouch and carries himself with a sense of confidence. His body language is assuring and poised. He comes across as a bold and inspiring leader. Modi understands that the tone impacts and often shapes communication and hence, he brings out his passion in his voice, especially while delivering speeches. He doesn't read his speeches in a monotone but speaks spontaneously with a broad outline, appearing interested in the matter at hand. This gives the people a sense of connection and reflects Modi's understanding of commonality.

He has a way of connecting with the rich and the poor, the liberal and the conservative alike. William J. Antholis, in his book, *India's most admired and most feared politician: Narendra Modi,* writes, "In person, Modi comes across as an effective administrator, a proud Indian nationalist, and a committed if not zealous Hindu. He also is a policy maven—introverted, precise, and even passionate about the most technical of subjects." His personality exudes his ideas and gives a reflection of his manner of work, along with steady confidence and charm. The iconic Hollywood costume designer Edith Head once said, "You can have anything you want in life if you dress for it."

Narendra Modi certainly dresses for it. His sartorial choices are a brand in itself today. His colorful half sleeved wrinkle-free *kurtas* and trimmed beard are a rage amongst the fashion conscious. However, his elegant appearance is only the tip of the iceberg. A self- made man, he has the vision and the ability to achieve it. Armed with a strong personality and voice, he seemingly has come up with his projected image as just the leader India needs.

Footsteps – Bob Marley

"Some people feel the rain. Others just get wet."

~ *Bob Marley*

Robert Nesta "Bob" Marley was a Jamaican reggae singer-songwriter, musician, and guitarist who achieved international fame and acclaim. He started out in 1963 with the group- the Wailers and created a distinctive songwriting and vocal style that would resonated with audiences worldwide. After the group disbanded in 1974, he pursued a solo career and went on to release the album Exodus which made him one of the world's best-selling artists of all time.

He was also an international icon for peace, love, and working towards better politics. A Rastafarian, songwriter, singer, and musician, Marley donned many hats and pulled off each role with finesse. In this he can be compared with Mr. Modi who too has a multidimensional personality. Marley had a vision, which he sang about, and his music transcended the boundaries of cultures and classes. India, the land of pluralities too needs a leader who can, while ensuring individual identities to the diverse religions and culture, lead to a collective identity for the nation.

Bob Marley brought about an iconic inclusion in global music by raising issues of poor and those who suffer. He shook the public consciousness through his words and music. The central theme of his songs had humans and their characters at the centre. Modi's political discourses and his governance is similarly centred around those at the bottom of the pyramid. His ideology is that of Integral Humanism which was propounded by the founder of Jansangha, Pt. Deen Dayal Upadhyaya, and the same has been adopted by BJP as its core ideology. Keeping humans at the centre and developing systems for larger good which rise above personal gains has indeed been Narendra Modi's core philosophy. If one closely analyses the governance style of Modi, it can be clearly observed that Modi follows a typical bottoms-up approach or an approach which begins with a person who is at the bottom of the pyramid and how the systems can be eased for him. This is quite similar to what Bob Marley propounded in his songs when he would detail on the misery and challenges of downtrodden people of the Africa or other parts of the world.

Influences in Marley's life came from heredity, and contributed to his optimistic psychological development. Family and social issues greatly affected Marley's thinking. In all his endeavors, he was motivated to contribute something great to this world. Modi's personality too was shaped greatly be his urge to do something great for his nation. Marley quit school, worked at a wedding shop, and spent the rest of his time working on vocals and music.

Both Bob Marley and Narendra Modi have distinctive personality traits which was helpful in creating a separate place for them in their respective fields. Bob Marley stood out in crowd due to his music and presentation. He entered the music scenes when the world was passing through a rather chaotic phase of rediscovery of human charter and materialistic benefits. That was an era when the western world was making an attempt to rediscover its roots and the concept of hippies and others was catching the fancy of the common person on the street. Bob Marley's music provided a direction and consoling factor of assimilation to many in his generation. Modi took charge of India when India was suffering from one of the worst social and economic crises. The public outcry against corruption, nepotism and political degeneration was at the peak and the Indian masses were looking for new and component leadership to steer them through such a situation. Narendra Modi, like in Bob Marley's famous song *Stand Up For Your Rights,* represents the success of a person who has risen from the bottom through sheer hard work and dedication, and who in many a sense defies the set norms needed for political success like family name, money and power, etc.

He started small but kept his love and ambition for music alive. Modi too had patience for formal schooling and spent his time strategizing and working for his dream to lead the country. Marley once said, "Though the road's been rocky, it sure feels good to me." This statement clearly showcases his optimistic outlook and reminds one that life's about enjoying every moment and making the most out of it.

13 | Risk-taking

"Only those who risk going too far can possibly find out how far they can go." ~ TS Eliot

Risk-taking is a critical part of leadership, and indispensable for a successful leader. Leaders who have made a difference have the courage to take a plunge when they saw a viable opportunity, instead of waiting for the 'right time'. This willingness to take risk is because these leaders are aware that being indecisive and extra cautious might kill the opportunity. However, taking a risk doesn't imply reckless behaviour. Effective leaders take calculated risks; they analyze the situation, their internal and external strengths and weaknesses, opportunities and threats, and then work to find out the best way to achieve results.

An important point of taking risks is the persistent desire by great leaders to think and do beyond the obvious. Any great leader who has left a mark on future has been not only taking risks but also learning from his actions and improvising on the actions which gradually leads to greater success and achievements. In many contexts, risk taking by a great leader can be attributed to his desire to bring about a positive change in systems and world around them. Abraham Lincoln epitomises the persistence of risk and success. He lost eight elections, suffered two business delinquencies, a nervous breakdown and extreme hardships before finally becoming the US President. He took risks and with continued passion and persistence, was successful in the end.

Especially in the modern world where innovation and creativity are paving ways for better opportunities, it has become imperative for leaders to allow themselves and their organizations to model new, relevant changes. This could only be possible if the leader has the foresight to look at an opportunity and know that it'll lead to development and hence, take the risk. Leaders need to be fearless in order to take risks and incorporate new ideas, for the fear of failure is what keeps them from experimenting.

Apart from the election of Narendra Modi being termed a 'calculated risk' by the Indians, it can also be observed that Modi himself is a risk-taker. He has displayed his understanding of the value of decisiveness and risk-taking in Indian politics by fighting to become a Prime Ministerial candidate, risking losing the safety of his position in Gujarat.

When Modi first took command of Gujarat as its Chief Minister, his agenda for growth was criticised by many. Though the call for development-based model of governance was advertised by political parties but it remained more of a colloquial terminology that anything else. Most political parties in India rather used it casually without detailing the finer aspects of it. The Modi governance model indeed for the first time, defined and underlined the developmental-based model of governance, at the bottom of which lay economic prosperity and growth. The developmental based model of governance indeed had its own challenges in context of communication and delivery and many a governments in India lost power when they tried projecting themselves as developmental government rather than a welfare government. The most apt example of the same of was with his own party, BJP's NDA government, which undertook a massive developmental-oriented model but was overtly defeated when it tried projecting the same through India Shining campaign. A common mentality of benchmarking and ignoring the gains while concentrating on what one has not got is to fret over the very dynamics of such a model. Despite the historical challenges, Modi took the risk and remained focussed on the developmental agenda, fully convinced that economic prosperity would indeed create a separate set of understanding among his target audience who would support and be benefitted by such an agenda. His risk thus paid off remarkably with Modi ruling the state of Gujarat for 15 years and ensuring that BJP becomes a reckoning force in the region. His model and results of risk have become benchmarks for states across India who are in some way or the other following his model of growth and development.

Risk-taking as a leader involves considering the people and the organization and then looking at, and acting upon, opportunities for possible development. Modi in his new role has plans that involve a lot of risk-taking, mainly because those opportunities have not yet been taken advantage of. As Prime Minister, his agenda mostly revolves around implementation of creative policies aiming at inclusion. Deviating from the manner of work set by the previous governments and issuing his own set of rules and work methods, Modi has clarified that he believes in his ideas to work efficiently and expects the risk to work out well. Delegating duties, empowerment of ministers, regulating work methods; all these require a certain kind of mindset surrounding the facet of risk-taking.

Jim Collins in his book, *Good to Great* mentions how complacency in decisions will only get you so far. "Good is the enemy of great," he observed. In order to utilize the full potential, leaders need to take initiative and encourage risk-taking among the people as well. Sticking to "good" would ultimately lead to organizational inertia and stagnation. True, there is risk of failure as well, but rare when the decision has been thought out properly and the risk is a calculated one. Modi as an optimist has an inclination towards risk-taking, and his intelligence enables him to consider all relevant aspects. This results in a decision for action that has potential of bearing fruit. Take the example of The Ministry of Department of North East Region (DoNER), created in 2001 during Atal Behari Vajpayee's reign as Prime Minister and responsible for all matters relating to the planning, execution and monitoring of development schemes and projects of the North-Eastern states. DoNER soon lost its relevance up until Modi brought it to light. Modi has handed the DoNER ministry to General V.K. Singh, a retired official. This is a calculated risk from his side, appointing an aggressive former military chief aiming to turn around a waning ministry.

Modi's emphasis on involving the neighbouring South Asian countries in the strategic planning for problem resolution of the North-Eastern states is unconventional as well as path-breaking. Another example would be the invitation of SAARC leaders to his swearing-in ceremony as the 15th Prime Minister of India. It is unusual, a strategic move and a risk. Modi has the sense to look at situations and find the best way to glean benefits from it. Within days of taking up as Prime Minister, Modi began by implementing changes in the bureaucratic structure that had been running in a fixed way since years. This risk apparently is successful, as his amendments are appreciated and making the officials happy. He has also encouraged bureaucrats to think creatively and take risks to overcome administrative paralysis that has set in over the past decade.

Simply acting on a whim works only with luck, and that is not Modi's way. In order to instil a culture of creativity, the leader must lead by example, allowing individuals to offer their own creative suggestions for doing things differently, and better. Risks must also be managed within the scope of an organization's ability to sustain possible damage, or tolerate change. Leaders like Modi recognize the importance of incorporating change and have to take decisions for doing so, most of which is risky. They need to consider the best way to execute those decisions to ensure positive returns. Novelist William Faulkner said, "You cannot swim for new horizons until you have courage to lose sight of the shore." That's how great leaders feel, and courageously make risky decisions, with focus on results.

While many would comprehend risk as a momentary decision-making ability, at the core of it lies a great degree of understanding of the ground realities and the personality of the leader. Often it's understood that a systematic person is rather risk averse, however, history is filled with examples that there lies a whole body of system for risk takers, the biggest being their conviction and ideologies. Narendra Modi is also known to be a person who places a lot of emphasis on systems and systems-driven approach. Hence, imagining him to be a risk taker might boggle the minds of a few. However, Narendra Modi comes from a background of dedicated ideology and self-conviction. Countering all the odds, he rose in the ranks of his party and life, but despite his growth, he still remained grounded. His ideology of supremacy which might be understood by many as a bit arrogant, indeed speaks of his strength of maintaining a high standard both for himself and for those around him. His risk taking is more systematic, aimed at strengthening the system, process and procedures around him, so that success becomes an inevitable by-product of his endeavour.

Footsteps - Steve Jobs

Leaders with the ability to take calculated risks dare to dream of what lies beyond the horizon and have the incentive to actually venture there and find out. One such risk-taker is inventor and CEO of Apple, Steve Jobs. He became one of the leading CEOs in the world because of his knack for risk-taking. Jobs had a keen eye and was able to foresee the future and power of computers and innovative technology. Armed with a belief in his ideas, he took the plunge and emerged as a global leader in technological innovation and world-class products. In a world that is essentially risk-averse, Jobs emerged as a pioneer of innovation, creativity and entrepreneurship.

Alan Deutschman, author of the book, *The Second Coming of Steve Jobs* wrote, "The big thing about Steve Jobs is not his genius or his charisma but his extra-ordinary risk taking." Jobs didn't even perform test-market runs for his products, trusting his own instincts and believing it'd do well. This level of risk-taking comes with a firm conviction in one's own capabilities and trust in their creations. Although Jobs's risk-taking might seem somewhat breakthrough, it sure was calculated. His products were such that would not have been understood unless they were brought out and marketed well. Jobs put across his ideas in the form of complete products and then created a market for those.

Delivering the commencement address at Stanford University in 2005, Steve Jobs stated, "Woz and I started Apple in my parents' garage when I was 20. We worked hard, and in 10 years Apple had grown from just the two of us in a garage into a $2 billion company with over 4000 employees. We had just released our finest creation – the Macintosh – a year earlier, and I had just turned 30. And then I got fired. How can you get fired from a company you started? Well, as Apple grew we hired someone who I thought was very talented to run the company with me, and for the first year or so things went well. But then our visions of the future began to diverge and eventually we had a falling out. When we did, our Board of Directors sided with him. So at 30 I was out. And very publicly out. What had been the focus of my entire adult life was gone, and it was devastating.

"I really didn't know what to do for a few months. I felt that I had let the previous generation of entrepreneurs down - that I had dropped the baton as it was being passed to me. I met with David Packard and Bob Noyce and tried to apologize for screwing up so badly. I was a very public failure, and I even thought about running away from the valley. But something slowly began to dawn on me — I still loved what I did. The turn of events at Apple had not changed that one bit. I had been rejected, but I was still in love. And so I decided to start over.

"I didn't see it then, but it turned out that getting fired from Apple was the best thing that could have ever happened to me. The heaviness of being successful was replaced by the lightness of being a beginner again, less sure about everything. It freed me to enter one of the most creative periods of my life. During the next five years, I started a company named NeXT, another company named Pixar. Pixar went on to create the world's first computer animated feature film, *Toy Story*, and is now the most successful animation studio in the world. In a remarkable turn of events, Apple bought NeXT, I returned to Apple, and the technology we developed at NeXT is at the heart of Apple's current renaissance. I'm pretty sure none of this would have happened if I hadn't been fired from Apple. It was awful tasting medicine, but I guess the patient needed it. Sometimes life hits you in the head with a brick. Don't lose faith. I'm convinced that the only thing that kept me going was that I loved what I did. You've got to find what you love. And that is as true for your work as it is for your lovers. Your work is going to fill a large part of your life, and the only way to be truly satisfied is to do what you believe is great work. And the only way to do great work is to love what you do. If you haven't found it yet, keep looking. Don't settle. As with all matters of the heart, you'll know when you find it. And, like any great relationship, it just gets better and better as the years roll on. So keep looking until you find it. Don't settle."

Narendra Modi is also self-confident, as is seen in the way he carries and presents himself, as well as in his public addresses. He trusts his own knowledge and probably that of his party-members, and makes decisions around the conviction that it'd bear fruit. He carries a reflection of Steve Jobs's risk-taking attitude and self-belief, which allows his actions to harbour sweet, and effective, results. He is a leader with a proactive approach, always at the forefront, learning and understanding the environment and then taking decisions that contribute towards the accomplishment of his goals. Modi does this not just by himself, but by encouraging and motivating the people to fearlessly follow the same.

14 | Decisiveness

"Nothing is more difficult, and therefore more precious, than to be able to decide."
~Napoleon Bonaparte

In her article titled *Great Leaders are Great Decision Makers,* leadership expert Larina Kase states, "When we think of what makes someone a great leader, one characteristic that comes to mind is decisiveness. We do not envision successful leaders standing around appearing unclear and uncertain. Instead, we view them as people who are able to quickly arrive at their decisions and communicate the goals to others."

Writing in a Harvard Business Review article titled *A Leader's Framework for Decision Making,* authors David Snowden and Mary Boone writes, "Good leadership requires openness to change on an individual level. Truly adept leaders will know not only how to identify the context they're working in at any given time but also how to change their behaviour and their decisions to match that context. They also prepare their organization to understand the different contexts and the conditions for transition between them."

The ability to analyze a situation and make sound decisions in a timely manner is one way of describing 'decisiveness'. A decisive leader makes effective, timely and well-informed decisions as well as creates an environment that fosters a confident and decisive way of thinking by individuals. Decisiveness is one of the key traits that enable successful leaders to exploit opportunities and as is said, 'strike when the iron is hot.' Decision making usually involves a good understanding of the organization's values and its strengths and weaknesses, as well as dealing with risk. The leader needs to have the ability to identify those risks and payoffs and make an informed decision. Such leaders need to possess courage and authority as well, for without these, they'd be dependent on others to make a decision. The leader must be independently capable of taking others' opinions into account when needed, and make choices themselves.

Decisive leaders gain respect from their people as they come across as confident, authoritative personalities. They are competent, credible and trustworthy, qualities that make people confident about their leaders' abilities. Followers are drawn to leaders who provide clarity and direction. Narendra Modi represents decisiveness and good governance skills, both of which would be crucial as he heads the first government in thirty years where a single party had absolute majority. Modi's selection of the council of ministers also reflects his strategic thinking and decisiveness, as it has been done in a way that augurs well for the future. This confidence and clarity of thought works as an assurance to the people that matters would be controlled and appropriate decisions taken.

There is information-overload in our world today, which makes it easy for leaders to fall into paralysis and procrastinate decision-making. It is important to have a good understanding of people and processes and stay proactive in their approach. Decisive leaders can grasp opportunities, identify potential problems and quickly modify and come to an appropriate decision. Timely decisions are valued and rewarded. Narendra Modi has vowed to end administrative chaos so deeply ingrained in the government system, portraying himself as a decisive man of action and one who is capable of bringing efficiency.

Decisiveness also involves allowing responsibilities to be delegated and encouraging decision-making from the lower levels. However, besides providing sufficient scope for workers' inputs, the leader should not entirely depend upon them or else they risk seeming pliable and non-assertive. Accepting responsibility as Prime

Minister, he has already started work to break through the governmental gridlock. On the eve of his swearing-in, he provided his ideas on the 'rationalisation' of the administrative system, stating that improvements in coordination, effectiveness and speed of decision-making would be made. Timely decisions enabled him to generate confidence among people that India would be able to kick-start growth, create jobs and tunnel through the path of development.

Modi also has some tough economic as well as creative decisions to make and there is faith that he'd be able to perform a balancing act. He has proposed to raise FDI in defence sector to 100 per cent, as well as considering bringing changes to FDI in other sectors such as railways, infrastructure and construction, in order to bring about an economic boost to the country. More recently, when Chinese President Xi Jinping visited India, Chinese incursion in Chumar, Ladakh, took place. That was a jolt for India and taking advantage of the President meeting him during the same time, Modi sharply asked him to withdraw his troops, no less than four times. To the people, Modi means dynamism, decisiveness and development, which is what they want after suffering through the policy paralysis of the previous government. Modi understands this sentiment and publicly talks about how nobody in the country accepts responsibility. He has stated that to bring the country out of this gloomy place, decisive decisions need to be taken. Enacting his vision of shining Gujarat and impressing Indians, he portrayed himself as the holder of efficiency and decisiveness.

In the face of a crisis, the problem will never navigate itself. Decisive leaders are aware of the fact that mistakes might be made, so they plan ahead, tackle problems as they come along and galvanize their teams into action. Way back in (year) when Tata decided to relocate his Tata Nano dream project from Singur, it is said that Modi acted with superhuman speed and got the Memorandum inked within 96 hours of Tata's announcement. He is known to take quick decisions and communicate those well on time. This single-window clearance is also a reason why investors flock to Gujarat, as it brings efficiency to the competitive business environment. It is not just about identifying opportunities, but also about quick decisions and action.

Modi has displayed a high level of decisiveness in both demanding and common situations. An important aspect of democratic governance is the challenge to manage the democratic aspirations and aligning them with the overall agenda of the government. Unlike a communist or socialistic form of governance where there is little leverage for the masses or the need by the government to consider issues of public, a democratic governance system requires keeping to the core the citizen aspect. This could lead to decision paralysis many a times, as was evident in several regimes of the past when even the Prime Minister of the country was either forced to leave the decision pending and suspended (leading to governance chaos) or take decisions under influence, both of which indeed did more harm than good for the nation and rule of law. People who have worked closely with Narendra Modi vouch for the fact that Narendra Modi takes definitive decisions and is pretty clear on the course of action that needs to be undertaken for proper implementation of his decision.

Napoleon had written, "Take time to deliberate, but when the time for action has arrived, stop thinking and go in." Decisiveness does not stop at making a decision; leaders need to ensure they're acted upon.

Footsteps - Margaret Thatcher

Margaret Thatcher is the only woman in British politics to become prime minister. Dubbed the Iron Lady by a Soviet Union journalist, she was the longest serving prime minister in the country's history and was well-known for her decisive leadership. She came to power after the 1979 general election and spent 11 years as Prime Minister before resigning in 1990. As Prime Minister, she implemented policies that have come to be known as Thatcherism. Often spoken of as extraordinary, Thatcher was brimming with passion, self belief and unconventional wisdom. She brought about sweeping economic changes that left an indelible impact on Britain.

Speaking on the issue of challenges facing her and the decisiveness of her regime, Thatcher in 1990 retorted, "This year the world seems to have relived the opening sentence of A Tale of Two Cities: it was the best of times, it was the worst of times. The worst of times as a tyrant struck down a small country that stands at the gateway to the Gulf; the best of times as tyranny crumbled and freedom triumphed across the continent of Europe. The toppling of the Berlin Wall. The overthrow of Ceausescu by the people he had so brutally oppressed. The first free elections in Eastern Europe for a generation. The spread of the ideas of market freedom and independence to the very heart of the Soviet Leviathan.

"Who could have foreseen all this? Who will ever forget the testimonies of courage we heard yesterday in this very hall? Our friends from Eastern Europe reminded us that no force of arms, no walls, no barbed wire can for ever suppress the longing of the human heart for liberty and independence. Their courage found allies. Their victory came about because for forty long, cold years the West stood firm against the military threat from the East. Free enterprise overwhelmed Socialism. This Government stood firm against all those voices raised at home in favour of appeasement. We were criticised for intransigence. Tempted repeatedly with soft options. And reviled for standing firm against Soviet military threats. When will they learn? When will they ever learn? Now again in the sands of the Middle East, principle is at stake. Mr. President, dictators can be deterred, they can be crushed they can never be appeased. These things are not abstractions. What changed the world and what will save the world were principle and resolve."

In a similar way, detailing the challenges faced by him as a Prime Minister and his commitment to resolve them, Narendra Modi in his Independence Day Address to the nation from Red Fort, said, "When I came to Delhi and noticed an insider's view, I felt what it was and I was surprised to see it. It seemed as if dozens of separate governments are running at the same time in one main government. It appeared that everyone has their own fiefdom. I could observe disunity and conflict among them. One department is taking on the other department, and taking on to the extent that two departments of the same government are fighting against each other by approaching Supreme Court. This disunity, this conflict among people of the same country! How can take the country forward? And that is why I have started making efforts for razing those walls; I have started making efforts at making the government, not an assembled entity, but an organic unity, an organic entity, a harmonious whole- with one aim, one mind, one direction, one energy. Let's resolve to steer the country to one destination. We have it in us to move in that direction."

Thatcher's decisiveness and strength of character is

reflected in Narendra Modi, the man of the moment. Like Thatcher, he is an assertive, nationalist, authoritarian and dynamic individual. The similarities don't end here. Both arose to the political world from grass root levels. Just like Thatcher, Modi is well acquainted with the problems that a common man faces in real life. Both came from families of lower-middle class grocers are united in their shared aspirations and dreams. Both were initially scoffed at by the elitists and faced derision but they stood her ground and managed to turn around the economic fortunes of their respective constituencies: Britain for Margaret Thatcher and Gujarat for Narendra Modi.

But it wasn't easy. When Thatcher became Prime Minister, Britain was in the midst of a long and crippling recession — powerful unions, uncompetitive businesses and a large Government. But Thatcher, a rank outsider with a nonconformist approach to conventional politics and economics proved that unions could be challenged and competitiveness restored. She focused on making government the enabler rather than controller. Narendra Modi too has inherited an economy that is facing the problems of slow growth, higher CAD and high inflationary pressures. But with his declaration of 'less government, more governance', reduced state involvement, focus on market economics and foreign investment, he may achieve what Thatcher did for Britain.

He has already managed to win a decisive mandate

on the back of combined aspirations of economic development irrespective of caste, religion and class to growth, development and jobs. He certainly has the charisma and ability to accomplish an economic turnaround.

15 | Empowerment

"You have to enable and empower people to make decisions independent of you. As I've learned, each person on a team is an extension of your leadership; if they feel empowered by you they will magnify your power to lead." ~ *Tom Ridge*

The move to empower citizens redefines the country. Despite the presence of powerful roadblocks to change, successful leaders act on the belief that participation by the people is the most compelling strategy for designing and implementing lasting change. Increased participation in governance will also lead to clarity in vision of freedom and democracy. This helps create a genuine democracy that nurtures progress and development. By enabling citizens, leaders help them take calculated risks. This helps citizens utilize their strengths and maximize the benefits to themselves and the community.

Empowering leaders believe in and place a high value on individuals and their opinions. They encourage critical thinking and in turn get blessed with highly innovative, motivated followers. They understand the economics of empowerment: empowered followers are also the most effective.

Narendra Modi too is an empowering leader which makes him highly effective. He understands the old Chinese philosophy which says that, *"give a man a fish, and you feed him for a day; show him how to catch fish, and you feed him for a lifetime"*.

Narendra Modi's model of Minimum Government, Maximum Governance underlines his ideas of running the state of affairs. Borrowed heavily from the concept of Integral Humanism as was propounded by Pt. Deen Dayal Upadhyaya, Modi's initiatives of transparency, efficiency and accountability has the sole aim of people's empowerment. While many question his strict discipline and a demanding attitude from his colleagues and bureaucrats, and think them to be not completely in line with empowerment as it sometimes leads to centralisation, yet a close analysis of his working style clearly elaborates on the fact that his governance style is indeed result driven and his concept of empowerment flows from the bottom. The model thus gives precedence to the citizens and common masses over the people managing the affairs of the state. Coming from a humble background, Modi has a first-hand experience of challenges being faced by common masses and how a model of empowerment from bottom would indeed strengthen the overall democracy of India, and thus his model is close to what Bill Gates mentioned in his commencement address at the Stanford University, "If we're going to make our optimism matter to everyone and empower people everywhere, we have to see the lives of those most in need. If we have optimism, but we don't have empathy – then it doesn't matter how much we master the secrets of science, we're not really solving problems; we're just working on puzzles."

As the great philosopher Chanakya once said, "Good Governance is achieved when government is the chariot and citizens are the charioteers. Modi through his policy of minimum government, maximum governance, advocates that the sole way of improving governance is by increasing citizens' role in governance. He opines that by empowering citizens and reducing the discretionary power of politicians, a healthy balance between authority and accountability can be created.

He has a similar policy for business. On various occasions, he has said that government should focus on its core activity of providing public goods and regulating the markets in a transparent and objective manner. He believes that government should not engage in activities that the private sector can perform in a more efficient manner, and should serve as an enabler for businesses to flourish. This approach can lead to a lean, efficient and responsive government.

Narendra Modi has demonstrated the benefits of empowering leadership in Gujarat. Under his leadership, the Gujarat government has consistently worked towards facilitating and promoting businesses and has invested extensively in building infrastructure. The government follows a transparent, rule-based industrialization process to protect the right of businesses and define their responsibilities. The Vibrant Gujarat Summit, organized to provide one stop service to potential investors is one of the state's famous initiatives. Gujarat government also operates corporations of strategic value to the overall welfare of the state-fertilizers, irrigation, gas, power, port and industrial development in a highly professional manner.

Modi seeks to empower government at all levels. He believes in restoring adequate authority and decision making power to the states acting on the principle of cooperative not coercive federalism. Federalism is a system based upon democratic rules and institutions in which the power to govern is shared between national and provincial/state governments, creating what is often called a federation. Cooperative federalism is a concept of federalism in which national, state, and local governments interact cooperatively and collectively to solve common problems, rather than making policies separately clashing over a policy in a system dominated by the national government. The 9th plan says, "*The essence of co-operative federalism is that the Centre and the State Governments should be guided by the broader national concerns of using the available resources for the benefit of the people. Co-operative federalism encourages the Government at different levels to take advantage of a large national market, diverse and rich natural resources and the potential of human capabilities in all parts of the country and from all sections of the society for building a prosperous nation.*".

Modi has said that the centre-state relationship should not be one of subjugation but collaboration. He believes that all forms of government are equal partners in delivering a better India. He believes that the State and Centre must unite over their welfare policies to maximize benefits to citizens. He has always stood for the principle of subsidiary - similar to decentralization - which advocates granting more autonomy to forms of government that are closer to people. In India, this should begin from the panchayat level.

Gujarat government's Chalo Taluke campaign is one such project. The Gujarat government, for this project, has allocated individual budgets for each panchayat and empowered them to decide on the needs in their respective villages. Senior officials and ministers were also part of the planning process ensuring collaboration with the state. Narendra Modi elaborated on the objective behind the project by saying, "State government wishes talukas to have beautiful schools, have its people empowered enough to fight malnutrition, have units for water management and not a single family living below poverty line".

Ever since Modi became Prime Minister, he has been trying to implement his ideas for empowerment. He believes in beginning from a smaller level, by making the citizens themselves believe that they have the power to change the situation in the country. MyGov, the website portal created for citizens to discuss and talk about relevant issues, giving them a voice, is one such example. Another example is the constant encouragement he provides to the youth of the country. Applauding the talent nurtured in IITs, Modi urged them to cultivate 'the science of thinking and the art of living' in its students, encouraging them to provide innovative solutions to problems faced by people in the country. He realizes the talent pool of people, and has openly displayed his trust in them. To empower them to come up with solutions, Modi has also thrown a challenge to IITs and asked them to help reduce India's dependence on imports for defence and security equipment like currency ink and tear gas. He stated that he believes India is very much capable of producing such products in the country.

Apart from defence equipment, he urged the students to look for solutions in the health sector, infrastructure and housing sector – by building technology that will enable rapid construction of structurally sound and economically viable houses – railways and other sectors. He has asked the 16 IITs to collaborate with industries so they can channelize the corporate social responsibility (CSR) funds into research. By way of such talks and motivation, Modi gives out a clear message: he believes in the power and talent of the people and would be willing to support them; they have the power. They just need to dedicate themselves to achieving what will be great for the Indian economy. Modi is also actively trying to understand reasons for the IITs not making it to the top 100 universities in the world. Recognizing the need to empower institutes of higher education, he urged the respective ministry to draw a road map for governance in line with the best global practices and to implement it without delay.

Footsteps - Bill Gates

"As we look ahead into the next century, leaders will be those who empower others".

~Bill Gates

William Henry "Bill" Gates, III is an American business magnate, philanthropist, investor, computer programmer, and inventor. Gates is the former chief executive and chairman of Microsoft, the world's largest personal-computer software company, which he co-founded with Paul Allen.

He believed in putting the right information into the hands of the people that can make the most of it. He said, "The vision is really about empowering workers, giving them all the information about what's going on so they can do a lot more than they've done in the past."

While he could have easily enjoyed success and concentrated on just the core business enterprise, Bill Gates was committed to create greater equality in society and saw Information Technology as one of the mediums for this. He was well aware that often any new endeavour could result in creating newer kinds of societal discrepancies and thus was committed to addressing them. In his own words, "By the 1990s, we saw how profoundly personal computers could empower people. But that success created a new dilemma: If rich kids got computers and poor kids didn't, then technology would make inequality worse. That ran counter to our core belief: Technology should benefit everybody. So we worked to close the digital divide. I made it a priority at Microsoft, and Melinda and I made it an early priority at our foundation – donating personal computers to public libraries to make sure everyone had access."

In this, he is quite similar to Narendra Modi who too believes in the concept of empowering or transformational leadership to change the fate of the nation. Both leaders showed ambition and genius from a very young age as they went on to achieve greatness in a short span of time. Another parallel is their love for research and innovation as a way to drive impact.

Another quality that both leaders share is their humility. As Microsoft became more successful, Bill Gates realized that he needed help managing the company. His vision, enthusiasm, and work were the driving force behind the company's rapid growth but he recognized the need for professional management and brought in Steve Ballmer, who later became indispensable to the organization. Modi too depends on his team and gives them the authority to make decisions, even though he sometimes comes across as an authoritarian. He handpicked the people who would be in the Prime Minister's Office. Both these leaders combine their passion and unyielding determination with a well structured team to achieve their visions.

Both believe that leaders should build the platform people can build on. One shouldn't just solve a one off problem. They believe in making the solution systematic, repeatable, and scalable.

They also share an authoritative style of leadership and the ability to mobilize people towards a well articulated vision. And even though both wield significant authority, they allow followers to figure out the best way to accomplish their goals. Bill Gates successfully moved Microsoft towards advancement just as Modi has led Gujarat and is leading India.

16| Patriotism

"Patriotism means to stand by the country. It does not mean to stand by the president or any other public official, save exactly to the degree in which he himself stands by the country."
~ Theodore Roosevelt

The root of the concept of patriotism lies in the devotion to one's country and an attachment to the culture of the country. People who harbour sentiments of patriotism feel strongly for issues pertaining to their country and strive for action to improve conditions in the country. For political leaders, patriotism is more than just a general leadership quality. It is a desirable characteristic if one is looking forward to lead the country. People look for patriotic leaders who do not simply call for mass promises but are also sincere and determined in their ideas of transformational changes. A true patriotic leader stands with honour and dignity and leads for justice to the people.

Considering patriotism in leadership, it can be thought of as a cultural expression. Effectively, patriotic leaders are able to transfer such feelings in their environment as well, and so people share a set of common beliefs and usually reach common agreements in decisions pertaining to the welfare of the organization or the country. Patriotic leaders are committed to their purpose, work hard, believe in their work and feel a sense of excitement for the organization. However, it is not just because of pure patriotic feelings that leaders strive hard to achieve goals. Patriotism simply gives them an added reason to feel satisfied about their work and think of creative ideas to make things even better. It is also closely associated with nationalism, especially in the case of political leaders.

Narendra Modi is a patriotic leader, concerned for the well-being of the Indian economy and development. This attachment propels him to embark on productive and creative thinking, which has the potential to bring about a solution to the awry state of affairs in the country. Modi's patriotism is not narrow-minded or exclusive, as is evident from his rigorous promotion of inclusive policies. Despite being known as a Hindu nationalist, he has spoken on the importance of equality and developing policies that include people belonging from all religious sects and caste.

An important differential factor in Narendra Modi's patriotism is that it's not just a by-product of his ideologies or is pure rhetoric in nature, rather, it aims at instilling the character and vision of the leader whose quest of patriotism is finitely translated into growth and empowerment for all. It is close to what the famous Australian Libertarian Prime Minister Robert Menzies stated in his iconic speech *The Forgotten People*, "To discourage ambition, to envy success, to have achieved superiority, to distrust independent thought, to sneer at and impute false motives to public service - these are the maladies of modern democracy. Yet ambition, effort, thinking, and readiness to serve are not only the design and objectives of self-government but are the essential conditions of its success."

His calls for Made in India or revisiting India's proud legacies to those that address the basic issues of cleanliness are reflective of his patriotism and desire to make India a reckoning force in the global arena.

For a country to experience sustainable development or nation-building, it is important for both, leaders and citizens to possess patriotism. Indian citizens had been craving for a stable government and a leader who'd possess the power to set the wheels of change in motion. During the Indian General Elections 2014, voting for Modi was called 'an act of patriotism'. Now that Modi holds power, he shoulders the expectations of millions of Indians who see in him the zest, courage and resolve to begin the very change that India needs.

One of the characteristics of a patriotic individual is having serious and deep concern for the issues of one's country, as well as possessing the will power and determination to bring about a positive change. "Pride" is also associated with patriotism, which is quite evident in Modi. While it is true that pride isn't necessarily a good trait, it is also true that it allows one to have a sense of self-assurance and confidence that is extremely necessary for individual development and the progress of the country.

Modi's concern and sensitivity to the state of affairs in his homeland has been developing since his formative years. Born in a lower middle class family in a nondescript town in Gujarat, Modi was particularly sensitive to the social and political developments around him. Nilanjan Mukhopadhyay in his book *The Man, The Times: Narendra Modi* brings up this description of Modi in the year 1956 when he was a six year old. At that time, Modi tried to participate in the movement for the separate state of Gujarat by running around distributing badges. Then in 1962 as a teen, he supplied tea to Indian soldiers on the war front. Subsequently, being in the midst of politics and RSS, Modi's ideology and behaviour got even more influenced towards patriotism. Once Modi began taking up responsibilities, his actions and decisions started having an influence on the nature of politics, society and the country.

Now leading the country as Prime Minister, Modi stated that India's socio-economic and political decline was mostly caused by the absence of pride on the part of the leaders. He aims to overcome this shortcoming by way of communicating to the citizens about the importance of being sensitive to changes around them and always striving for development where there's scope for it. This is something he always intones in his public addresses, such as the one during Independence Day. In the hour-long speech, Modi introduced himself not as the *pradhan mantri,* but *pradhan sewak,* or the prime servant in the service of the country. He also recognized the importance of labourers, farmers, the youth and the women who have been instrumental in making India practice all that helped develop it. Remembering the martyrs who laid down their lives for the freedom of the nation, Modi stressed on taking measures to make India worth that sacrifice. He talked about the need to work on development in villages, educating the girl child, provision of basic sanitation facilities, and reducing poverty. He focused on communicating to the people that they need to move together towards development together, and in harmony for the betterment of the nation.

Speaking in an interview, Modi stated that he was a proud Hindu by faith but first and foremost he sees himself as an Indian. Modi is a patriot, a nationalist and most of all, ambitious for the nation; presently, just the kind of leader India needs.

Footsteps - Bal Gangadhar Tilak

History has numerous examples of great political leaders, characterized by the common trait of patriotism. Bal Gangadhar Tilak, a popular leader who fought for India's independence, is one example of a patriotic leader. Popularly addressed by the honorific 'Lokmanya,' meaning 'accepted by the people as their leader,' his ideals are of great relevance to the India of today.

Despite Tilak's Hindu conservatism, he was much influenced by Western thought on politics and metaphysics, also reflected in Modi. The emergence of Lokmanya Tilak in Indian politics was a watershed event as he brought with himself a new kind of leadership that was highly intellectual, with a clear vision and intense patriotism. At the same time, it had its roots in the vast illiterate and poor masses. Modi's policies based on inclusion are indicative of a similar sentiment. Tilak as a leader encouraged a broad perspective at a time when the British wanted to unify various regions for easier administration, and urged the citizens to think beyond their own regions and consider the country as a whole. His weeklies, Kesari and Mahratha played an important role in national awakening, imbibing patriotic feelings in the people. It also acted as an active force in a great social, political and cultural movement in India.

Tilak stressed on the need for personal efforts that steer the passion of nationalism. He famously put the nation first by stating, "Religion and practical life are not different. To take Sanyasa (renunciation) is not to abandon life. The real spirit is to make the country your family, work together instead of working only for your own. The step beyond is to serve humanity and the next step is to serve God."

Narendra Modi has similarly always opposed personal gains and has withstood against personal benefits by people in power. In the Indian political scenario where nepotism is highly prevalent and politicians and their families are known to take advantage of power, Narendra Modi has remained unscathed and his closest family still lives within their modest means. His patriotism is thus aimed at growth of the nation and not oriented towards his own personal growth or benefits to his family.

Tilak had worked tirelessly to bring about the unification of the country and believed in 'swaraj' (self-rule). He coined the popular slogan, 'Swaraj is my birthright and I shall have it,' bringing the basic Indian consciousness of freedom and independence to the forefront. Modi in his last election campaign stated that the elections themselves in a way have brought about a spark of change for good governance. Like Tilak, he is a proponent of swaraj and has reiterated that it is the right of people. In the present scenario, Tilak's model is a relevant one to follow, in order to overcome the policy paralysis set in the bureaucratic system.

Tilak's model of nationalism was aimed at creating a larger mass of integration and harmony among the participants. He opposed bifurcation of Bengal on linguistic and social basis and at the same time revived the dormant Ganesh Utsav for creating a massive social harmony. He followed an approach which connected with masses across India. Much like Tilak who was extremely proud of his country, legacy, culture and religion, Narendra Modi also carries his personal trait of nationalism up his sleeves. He has oft and again stated, "I would like to see myself as an Indian first and foremost. I am a Hindu by faith and I am proud of the faith I belong to. I love my country."

17| Networking

"If you want to go somewhere, it is best to find someone who has already been there"
~Robert Kiyosaki

Networking is about making connections and building enduring, mutually beneficial relationships. Meeting the "right" helps expand one's sphere of influence. As has been said many times: ultimately, it's not about who you know, but who knows you! An African proverb says, *"If you want to go fast, go alone; if you want to go far, go with others"*.

Also, relationships catalyze success. People do business with those whom they like and trust. Networking is the single most proficient, effective and enduring tactic in building relationships. To succeed, leaders continually connect with new people, cultivate mutually beneficial relationships and leverage their networks.

In the age of media, where individuals are bombarded with advertisements, emails, opinion broadcasts and sales pitches, messages get cluttered. Personal relationships can enable one to stand out, rise above the noise and remain in sight and mind. As Christine Comaford-Lynch said, *"Networking is marketing. Marketing yourself, marketing your uniqueness, marketing what you stand for"*.

Effective leaders master the art of three forms of networking: operational, personal, and strategic. The first helps them manage current internal responsibilities and accomplish work in an efficient manner, the second helps in personal and professional development and the third helps them figure out future priorities and challenges and the stakeholders they would need to enlist.

The importance of establishing connections to other powerful, intelligent people is extremely important in creating a successful political career. Political leaders can and will continue to learn the important aspects of career networking for themselves, their teams, and their constituencies. Sharing information and opportunities with colleagues has a synergistic effect. It increases supply of information and creates influential and powerful leadership. Leaders need to become better networkers to build successful careers and this requires global understanding and presence.

Narendra Modi has definitely mastered the art of networking with not only his peers, contemporaries and mentor but also the Indian electorate. He understands the leverage personal style can have for networking and based on the insight, he has created his own personal brand: NaMo. He also strategically plans his activities. Keeping in mind that not all networking events are equal, he chooses those which guarantee the best return on investment. This may explain why he has the affinity for business summits and seminars.

Throughout his life, he has demonstrated the benefits of systematically planned networking. He chose mentors after a great deal of evaluation and his futuristic moves have led to great connections. Keshavrao Deshmukh, Lakshmanrao Inamdar, Shankersinh Vaghela, Keshubhai Patel,and Nathalal Jhagda were some of the many powerful personalities who mentored him and accelerated his rise to power.

But relationships don't develop overnight. And Modi knows that well. He identifies who he wants to build relationships with and then invests time. In the book- Narendra Modi: The Man, The Times- Mr. Mukhopadhyay writes that Mr. Modi was adept at picking mentors. Nathalal Jhagda, the then organizing secretary of the Jan Sangh was one of his mentors. Modi even carried his luggage whenever Mr. Jhagda had to travel. With all his mentors he managed to forge a personal relationship based on reverence. As Dale Carnegie said, "You can make more friends in two months by becoming interested in other people than you can in two years by trying to get other people interested in you."

He also understood the importance of building a team of peers and subordinates and attracted talent by showing expertise and exuding power and confidence. Engaging meaningfully, remembering people and making sure that they remember him: Narendra Modi is well acquainted with the art of building lasting relationships. Maya Angelou said, *"I've learned that people will forget what you said, people will forget what you did, but people will never forget how you made them feel."* The train story by Leena Sarma- reminiscence of the time when she met Modi in a train and his show of chivalry and kindness towards a perfect stranger- epitomizes what Angelou had written.

Modi has been in touch with many leaders across the world ever since he acquired the post of Prime Minister of India. Attending conferences and meetings, inviting foreign delegates to the country, addressing the masses about the issues facing the world, Modi is doing everything in his capacity to connect at a larger level, to make his presence felt and to form strong political and diplomatic relations as he seeks to carve out a stronger role for India as a global player. His first foreign visits were to neighbouring Bhutan and Nepal, in a gesture of friendship and in a way to establish cross border relationships. He also asked the Foreign Minister Sushma Swaraj to visit Bangladesh and Afghanistan.

Another kind of networking that Modi has mastered is social networking. He identified social media as the channel that could lead to meaningful dialogue between the government and people and used it as a direct means of information that gave his party the much-needed local pulse. His victory message has become the most re-tweeted post in Indian history – more than 70,000 and counting. There were 58m tweets related to the elections between the start of 2014 and the announcement of Modi's victory, according to data published by Twitter India, with more than 2m posted on results day itself. He has also agreed to meet Mark Zukerberg, the founder of Facebook on his visit to India in October for India's first internet.org summit. The summit aims to make internet easily accessible to people across the globe, which is something that Modi strongly advocates in the context of India. He had also met Facebook's Chief Operating Officer Sheryl Sandberg earlier in July, recognizing that India is one of the biggest and important markets for the social media company.

It is important to mention that Modi's style of networking, if not just upwardly oriented, is rather multidirectional and reaching out to all his relevant stakeholders. His program *Mann Ki Baat* through All India Radio, which was aimed at reaching out to people in faraway villages and other places who do not have access to modern technologies like internet, became an instant hit and his desire for seeking suggestions from the listeners indeed resulted in a deluge of 5000-6000 letters on a daily basis. For those who could access internet, a separate forum was created on the website mygov.in for sharing the same. Unlike previous regimes, Modi's networking is not just confined to upper echelons of power but rather, it is more democratic and appreciative of the fact that in democracy, power flows from the people and not otherwise. It thus covers the intrinsic 360 degrees networking mechanisms and connect, which was missing in several previous regimes that India saw.

Footsteps - Warren Buffett

Robert Kiyosaki once said, *"The richest people in the world look for and build networks. Everyone else looks for work."* The quote doesn't just go for the richest but also the most powerful; and most of the times, riches and power go hand in hand.

Warren Edward Buffett, an American business magnate, investor, and philanthropist is an apt example. Widely considered as the most successful investor of the 20th century, he is the chairman, CEO and largest shareholder of Berkshire Hathaway and consistently ranked among the world's wealthiest people.

His passion for networking could be well understood by his own statements:

"It takes 20 years to build a reputation and five minutes to ruin it. If you think about that, you'll do things differently."

"It's better to hang out with people better than you. Pick out associates whose behavior is better than yours and you'll drift in that direction."

He understands the importance of the ability to build and nurture relationships. He has spoken about how people skills are critical and could take decades to master. Another important lesson to learn from the master is how investments are connected with business relationships. And of course, no talk on networking can be completed without talking of motivating subordinates with trust and accountability.

In their techniques of networking as well as the importance that they place on it, Buffett and Modi are quite similar. Both show consistency in the value they place on creating relationships.

This isn't the only quality they share though. Both have excellent communication skills. Buffett's ability to communicate with people at all levels of investment has been significant in according him the reputation of a financial genius.

Buffett believes that though going against the popular notion can be difficult, it's usually the only way to achieve success. Modi has on numerous occasions has swam against the tides only to turn it.

Also both believe in the might of internet and agree that with passion and resilience, internet can serve as the most powerful tool to accomplish greatness.

When Warren was in his 20's, he told his wife that one day they were going to be incredibly wealthy (despite having no real wealth at the time). He wasn't exactly sure when, but he was sure it was going to happen. He told her to prepare and think about what she'd do with a great deal of money. Then he slowly made $50 billion dollars. This story illustrates very intricately the power of dreaming big. And Modi dreams big. Both men have achieved what may have appeared impossible to most but then they haven't done what most have.

18 | Ambition

"A man's worth is no greater than the worth of his ambitions." ~ Marcus Aurelius

One of the hardest aspects of leadership is the ability to clearly focus and balance between personal ambition and those set for the organization. Ambition is the inner drive, or desire, for some distinctive achievement and the willingness to strive for its accomplishment. Successful leaders are known to harbour great ambition, which works as a driving force for their perseverance and compliment other leadership skills. Effective leaders exhibit a balanced combination of skills, personality and ambition that influences the people and inspires them to believe in the leader.

Ambition however, also has a negative connotation, as it is frequently mistaken for ego or the desire for power by sacrificing integrity and values. Successful, ambitious leaders possess ego, but those are channelled into their organizations and purpose, not for personal aggrandizement. Leaders with high ambition make decisions considering the long-term scenario and all stakeholders. It needs to be channelled into the process of making the organization better. What complicates matters is when such leaders as Narendra Modi come with a larger-than-life personality. He is considered a visionary and a game-changer, yet perceived to have ego, even though it might have been used in a constructive manner. Leaders cannot afford to project themselves as people who deny personal ambition, since it takes away the essence of individuality in leadership.

Modi is undoubtedly an ambitious leader, with great dreams for the country. Ambition is relatively inherent in an individual's personality, as is clearly reflected in Modi's personality. Even as a youngster having lower middle class roots, he knew that he wanted a distinguished name and position for himself. The desire to move forward, persevering despite the odds, and learning from every possible situation: these are some characteristics that indicate a leader motivated to fulfil his ambition. As Prime Minister, his ideas for development are quite ambitious; building 'a hundred new cities', extending a high-speed rail network across the subcontinent, making India a hub of investment activity, to name a few. He is also focusing on maintaining was for the first time in India that a democratic system of election for a leader took place in any political party. In almost all parties, power has remained confined to either the founder or his/her close family members and often the wishes of common workers stood ignored as the leaders were entrusted on them. Much like the primary model prevalent in USA where anyone could stand for the leadership position and is only nominated when he or she has garnered ample supporters, Modi's rise has brought about a remarkable model of internal democracy which was more or less absent from the Indian political system. Thus, his nomination within his own party and now as Prime Minister of India is not just a rise of an individual from the bottom circle of the political disposition, rather it also reflects upon ambition and aspirations of a common man on the street, which also includes grassroots political workers who have worked tirelessly but are often ignored in decision making and selection of their own leadership.

An important aspect of great leadership is that they have the unique talent of transferring and rubbing off their ambition to others. This rub off indeed create a critical mass which then transforms a personal ambition into a societal or national ambition. Gandhi, Kennedy, Martin Luther King, Abraham Lincoln etc. aptly transferred their ambition to people standing behind them. Modi has displayed this quality time and again. In his maiden independence day address to nation he said, "Today in ties with other countries, which is vitally important for economic and strategic reasons. Modi clearly has set for himself and his team, a very ambitious agenda.

Modi has been appreciated for a lot many things, including but not limited to his vision, determination and strategic thinking, yet his ambitions were made into a key campaign issue and he was relentlessly attacked for that. He attracted criticism for his promotion and the supposed 'raw pursuit of power', which shows the pessimist view of ambition perceived by the people. However, the country is entering a phase where there is more honest pursuit of power and the voter will probably not dismiss any politician based on his ambitions, but might as well chuck him out if he fails to deliver.

Bringing about changes when faced with high level of resistance is a trait effective leaders have, for they don't just have an idea in mind, but the drive and will to turn those ideas into reality. Such leaders are highly capable and possess a paradoxical mix of two important qualities: great ambition and humility. Their focus of ambition is not themselves, but the greater good. They're driven to achieve their vision set for the organization or in the case of Modi, the country. He has branded himself as an able politician. As ambition is closely intertwined with clarity of vision and decisiveness, Modi stands out as the one leader who doesn't have any castles in the air. He has declared his ambitions and goals clearly. It is rare in

Indian elections to see a candidate clearly state what he wants and what he hopes to achieve. Long-term planning and focus are his strengths, suitably displayed during the election campaign in 2014, the preparations for which he started more than a year before. Leading from the front is something he does naturally, firmly believing in 'walking the talk'. He is known to have put in 20 hours of work a day, hopping from venue to venue and addressing over 430 rallies.

Ambitious leaders feel the need to achieve their big dreams and create master plans to fulfil their purpose. They feel that without goals, they'd have no growth. This is one reason why such people have a knack for recognizing golden opportunities. They see ways to do things differently. It could be a new product, process or service. Ambition is also the driver that challenges assumptions. Questioning the stated methods stimulates debate and ultimately, action. This also enables a clear vision. Modi has a clear idea of what he wants to accomplish and does not look for ratification from the market.

Narendra Modi's ambition has often faced criticism due to political reasons, but he, as a prudent person, has always seized the opportunity that came his way. Many, including several of his own party-men, questioned the manner in which Narendra Modi was appointed the Prime Ministerial Candidate for his party. Probably it the face of global competition, when we have to realize the dreams of millions of Indians, the country cannot run on the lines of "it happens", "it goes". In order to fulfil the aspirations of masses, we have to sharpen the tool called the Government machinery, we have to make it keen, more dynamic, and it is in this direction that we are working. Brothers and Sisters, whether the citizens of the country should take steps for the welfare of the nation or not? You imagine, if this 125 crores of countrymen move one step forward, then the country moves 125 crore steps forward. The meaning of democracy is not just limited to electing a government, but its meaning is that 125 crore of citizens work together joining shoulder with the government to fulfill hopes and aspirations of the country, this is the meaning of democracy."

Footsteps – Abraham Lincoln

Abraham Lincoln, one of America's greatest heroes owing to his incredible impact on the nation, shares with Narendra Modi the story of a humble beginning and the rise to achieve the highest office. As a youngster, Lincoln's family lived a hard life, scraping a living and fighting for survival in Spencer County, Indiana. Nine year old Lincoln's mother succumbed to the milk sickness outbreak in 1818. Lincoln grew distant from his father, but maintained a loving bond with his step mother, a generous woman with three kids of her own. Despite being illiterate herself, she encouraged Abraham to read, and in a place where books were scant, he could be found walking miles in order to borrow a book.

To save themselves from another outbreak of the disease, the family later moved to Illinois. Abraham had always been ambitious, and despite the lack of money, friends and education, contested for Illinois General Assembly elections in 1832, at the age of 23. He lost, even though he received a good vote because of his eloquent speech. He decided to become a lawyer and for the most part, was self-taught. He was determined, and in his second campaign two years later, he won the election to the state legislature. As a lawyer, he participated equally in politics and in 1846, was elected to the US House of Representatives, from where he worked to abolish slavery. He was elected the President in 1860.

Much like Modi's call from the Red Fort of asking for support from the masses of India and addressing himself as the Prime Servant and not Prime Minister of India, Abraham Lincoln in his First Political Announcement at New Salem, March 9, 1832 stated, "Every man is said to have his peculiar ambition. Whether it be true or not, I can say for one that I have no other as great as that of being truly esteemed of my fellow men, by rendering myself worthy of their esteem. How far I shall succeed in gratifying this ambition is yet to be developed. I am young and unknown to many of you. I was born and have ever remained in the most humble walks of life. I have no wealthy or popular relations to recommend me. My case is thrown exclusively upon the independent voters of this county, and if elected, they will have conferred a favor upon me, for which I shall be unremitting in my labours to compensate. But if the good people in their wisdom shall see fit to keep me in the background, I have been too familiar with disappointments to be very much chagrined."

Abraham Lincoln had spent a considerable amount of time in state politics, working for the betterment of society according to what he saw – slavery. In the same vein, Modi spent years as Chief Minister of Gujarat, focusing on developmental aspects of the state under him, making the place a model state for the rest of the country. Both these leaders, driven by their ambition and powerful work, had created for themselves a huge base of supporters, before trying out for the ultimate position of power and authority.

19 | Self-discipline

"The first and best victory is to conquer self."
~ Plato, philosopher

In simple terms, self-discipline can be defined as the ability to force yourself to do something you know you should do, regardless of your impulses or desires. It is the willingness to overcome the natural urge to engage purely in fun, easy or quick ventures. Self-discipline isn't easy but it is the price one must pay for success. This is the reason why the most successful men and women possess self discipline and other common characteristics which can be nurtured with the practice of self-discipline such as hard work, integrity, ambition, risk-taking and patience.

In the words of Brian Tracy, the world renowned author and speaker, "Many people feel that they lack self-discipline in certain areas and they often assume that, *"That's just the way I am."* Are some leaders born with natural qualities and abilities that make self-discipline easy for them? It may be true that there are such things as natural born leaders, however most leaders are made by hard work and self-development. The fact is that you can develop whatever leadership styles and qualities that you consider desirable and necessary. For some people it will be easier, and for others it will take more time and effort. But each person has the inborn ability to shape his or her character and personality in a positive way by being clear about his or her future intent and determined enough to press forward through the difficulties, resistance, and setbacks."

Self-discipline helps to turn failure into success. When one attempts something and is greeted with failure, the basic instinct is to just give up. However, the self-disciplined will not give up and push on until they accomplish what they set out for. This ability pertains to the knowledge that failure is a step to success. To live a self-disciplined life, one should have the willingness to forego instant gratification and work towards long-term satisfaction. It is an act of cultivation that requires one to connect today's actions to future results. There is a season for sowing and reaping and self-discipline enables one to understand which is which.

Successful leaders have focused on first improving their own selves, understanding their strengths and weaknesses so as to be able to perform in the most perfunctory manner. Narendra Modi, the 15th Prime Minister of India and prior Chief Minister of Gujarat, is known to be self-disciplined and austere. India as a country needed a leader who'd not only be disciplined, but also would facilitate self-discipline in the country as a whole. As Prime Minister, Narendra Modi began with an attempt to inculcate self-discipline in the government; introducing deadlines, new systems of work, encouraging cleanliness and urging ministers to refrain from buying new cars. To kick-start what he calls will be India's renaissance – a transformation from a tourist nightmare into a citadel of Indian culture and civilization – he believes that self-discipline to get into the habit of cleanliness is the most important thing the citizens can do for the development of the country. The way ahead for India needs the strong will of people through self-discipline. The US had also made a national effort to make the country clean, which was as dirty as India in the 1950s. He understands that as a leader, it is his responsibility to practice what he preaches, as well as urging his people to do the same. His call for a clean India by 2019 seems doable now, what with advanced technology and newer means of spreading awareness and communication.

Being self-disciplined is a habit, a practice, a philosophy and a way of living. All great success in life is achieved through sustained efforts and a single-minded focus on the goal with a determination and resilience to accomplish it. All leaders achieve greatness by engaging in long, often unappreciated, hours, weeks, months and even years of concentrated, disciplined work in a particular direction. Modi, in his quest for attaining the coveted seat of Prime Minister, had a clear focus, a well-planned strategy and hours of hard work. This is evident from the way he managed his election campaign, putting in 20 hours of work a day and working tirelessly throughout. Even during his youth as well as the time when he was rising in his career, it was self-discipline that helped him be perseverant, focused, optimistic and energized. Self-discipline helped him recognize opportunities for what they were worth and helped him make good use of those as they came up.

A unique aspect of self-discipline is how much of it is entirely internal, and more personal than professional. It's an added benefit that self-discipline leads itself into helping one as a professional and a leader. Appreciators of Modi call him 'superhuman' and believe that he has some inherent inner power that could either be God-gifted or spiritual or acquired through years of self-discipline and hard work. As a youngster, Modi is known to have 'vanished' from home for days at a stretch and staying in places where no human habitation persisted. He might have felt the pressures of the country's social systems and found collaborating with different people wearing, thus looking for an outlet to revitalize him, reflecting on and bringing back his focus.

Self-disciplined leaders have the ability to distinguish high value tasks from the low value ones and thus are able to organize systems better and manage time and resources to the optimum level. Modi's government will be glimpsing an example of this as he delegates work and distributes responsibility, prioritizing and focusing on high value tasks. Authentic leadership is felt intensely, only when it is absent. Authentic leaders are recognized by their influence, impact, insight, initiative, knowledge and a clear sense of purpose, achieved with self-discipline. Modi certainly fits the description.

While self-discipline of individual could be a rather achievable target, rubbing off in one's governance style and across the system is indeed an onerous task. Modi demands high level of self-restraint and self-discipline from his colleagues and people working with him, which indeed has been a transition from the past. Previous regimes in India, partly due to the collation politics and desire to remain in power, and majorly due to lack of self-discipline, fell prey to several compromises which eventually impacted the governance levels and growth of the nation. Narendra Modi due to his definitive mandate and governance priorities has been successful in conveying to his colleagues and bureaucrats around him, often in strong terms, the need to remain cogged to the highest standards of self-discipline. He tends to follow the philosophy that societal discipline can only be achieved if every individual adheres to individual discipline which then can have a cumulative upward impact.

Footsteps – Aung San Suu Kyi

One of the world's most prominent political prisoners, Aung San Suu Kyi is a Burmese opposition politician and chairperson of the National League for Democracy (NLD) in Burma. When in 1990, the military refused to hand over power to her party, she was kept under house arrest for fifteen years in the period of 21 years, finally being released in 2010. Since then, she's received a number of awards including the Nobel Peace Prize in 1991. She chose non-violence and civil disobedience against the Burmese government and worked for better health and education facilities for the Burmese people, apart from democratization, human rights and freedom.

Suu Kyi had been self-disciplined even as a child, as it is accounted by her classmates, friends and teachers. She was a sincere student and disciplined in the manner of everyday life. It might have been because of her family's political background, which naturally made her inclined towards a life of hard work and discipline, since both her parents had been important political figures. Her speeches are reminders of the incredible power of passion and sincerity for productive results. Her determination, peaceful demeanour and self-discipline contribute towards her success. Despite all odds, it has been this discipline to organize her life and work, to persevere when everything was bleak, that made her such a symbol of inspiration.

People close to Narendra Modi vouch for his simplicity of life and strict personal discipline. Known to be extremely hard working, Modi's rise in Sangh and in his personal life can be attributed to his dedication and self-discipline. Narendra Modi's self-discipline is reflected in his simple lifestyle, his vegetarian diet and his passion for balancing his health and faith. An example of this can be seen in his recent visit to USA where he fasted during the holy days of Navratras, surviving on just water and lemon juice, despite having a treacherous schedule of meetings and engagements. Even as a youth, Narendra Modi would retire into seclusion to practice meditation and incrementing his will power.

In her famous speech, The Freedom from Fear, Su Kyi said, "The effort necessary to remain uncorrupted in an environment where fear is an integral part of everyday existence is not immediately apparent to those fortunate enough to live in states governed by the rule of law. Just laws do not merely prevent corruption by meting out impartial punishment to offenders. They also help to create a society in which people can fulfil the basic requirements necessary for the preservation of human dignity without recourse to corrupt practices. Where there are no such laws, the burden of upholding the principles of justice and common decency falls on the ordinary people. It is the cumulative effect on their sustained effort and steady endurance which will change a nation where reason and conscience are warped by fear into one where legal rules exist to promote man's desire for harmony and justice while restraining the less desirable destructive traits in his nature." She thus placed emphasis on a just and equitable system of governance and relative strength of human character. In a similar manner, Narendra Modi has emphasised on greater transparency and fearless services to the masses by his administration. Reaching out directly to people, propagating the governance model of "Sabka Saath, Sabka Vikas" (All together for mutual growth) and keeping a strong eye on the governance delivery, Narendra Modi is working to ensure that common masses of India are not subjected to any injustice and they have access to exceptional governance.

Like Su Kyi, Narendra Modi epitomises the strength of human character, as both have wilfully stood against odds, most notable being corruption bred from power. Both have highly nationalistic fervour and their dedication is beyond all explanation. Su Kyi displayed it when she declined to leave her country to see her terminally ill husband whom she met only five times in her married life, for she feared that if she left the country then she will never be allowed to return back to Burma, and fought for the rights of her countrymen. Displaying similar nationalistic feelings, Modi has time and again stood for maintaining the nationalistic character of India.

When Narendra Modi speaks, one can see a similar passion, even though for these two political figures, the background for that passion might be different. The essence is the same, however. With self-discipline comes the power to conduct oneself in the right manner, no matter the situation. As she addresses the people of Burma, the two things Aung San Suu Kyi wishes for them to demonstrate are self-reliance and self-discipline.

20 | Strategy

"What do you want to achieve or avoid? The answers to this question are objectives. How will you go about achieving your desire results? The answer to this you can call strategy."~ William E Rothschild

The word 'strategy' has its origin in military warfare. However, it also has a notorious reputation of being the most misunderstood, or transcending itself into an amoebic translation. People, and especially in corporate jargons, it is used rather casually with everything being stated as strategy. The key question thus arises - what exactly is strategy and is it really so complex to comprehend?

Russell Conwell in his iconic *Acres of Diamonds* speech stated an interesting methodology to understand it. He said, "Did you ever study the history of invention and see how strange it was that the man who made the greatest discovery did it without any previous idea that he was an inventor? Who are the great inventors? They are persons with plain, straightforward common sense, who saw a need in the world and immediately applied themselves to supply that need. If you want to invent anything, don't try to find it in the wheels in your head nor the wheels in your machine, but first find out what the people need, and then apply yourself to that need, and this leads to invention on the part of people you would not dream of before. The great inventors are simply great men; the greater the man the more simple the man; and the more simple a machine, the more valuable it is."

The strategy of success thus has simplicity at its base. Now simplicity can be translated and understood in many aspects. It could be simplicity of approach, simplicity of how one carries himself or simplicity of words.

An act which converted the simpleton Mohandas Karamchand Gandhi into Mahtama Gandhi was his simplicity and approachability. He was very well aware that India is a diverse nation of emotions and culture and the best method reach to the masses indeed was simplicity. His *khadi* and simple words became his hallmark. In fact in his book *My Experiments With Truth,* Gandhi himself admits that he had a limited vocabulary of around 3000 words, yet those 3000 words left a marked impact on the generations to come. He was as comfortable sitting in house of a poor cobbler as he was sitting in the Birla Mansion among the richest Indiana. Similarly, Narendra Modi delves on his intrinsic strength of displaying simplicity of approach and connecting with people from all walks of life.

Once simplicity and comfort of approach is achieved, then the next agenda that remains is developing a plan of action for achieving the set goals.

Achieving set goals is closely related to having a plan of action in the first place. The art of planning, prioritizing, setting smaller objectives and directing people in order to attain those objectives, is strategic planning. It is vital for any leader to have a well-formed strategy at any point of time. Strategy is what provides direction to the organization and helps make roles and responsibilities clear. To make this happen, the leader's job is to create and communicate a clear vision for the enterprise in such a manner that it engages the imagination as well as energies of the people. The leader must build both, an organizational culture and an organizational capability for executing strategy.

A leader thinks strategically in order to better understand the environment, the opportunities and resources available. The ability to anticipate, challenge, interpret, decide, align and learn, form the heart of strategic thinking. Perhaps the most recent and relevant example is Narendra Modi's election campaign. It is a perfect anecdote of how to prepare and successfully implement a marketing and branding campaign. His transformation from a regional politician to a decisive leader with a clear developmental agenda has 'strategy' at its core. Teams were created to take over his media strategy, a task force constituted to handle his campaigns in certain strategic areas, advertising agencies helped create slogans, advertising, radio and print campaigns. Modi has captured popular imagination with his well-formed strategy and its implementation, resulting in his landslide victory in the 2014 Lok Sabha elections.

The famous Indian strategist Chanakya mentioned in his book *Arthashastra*, "Before you start some work, always ask yourself three questions - Why am I doing it, What the results might be and Will I be successful? Only when you think deeply and find satisfactory answers to these questions, go ahead." Narendra Modi is known as the man of who has a clear objective whenever he is setting an agenda for himself. While many of his critics might try to attribute his success on singular aspects like public relations or his individual policy but a clear insight and in-depth analysis proves that there lies a whole body of coordinated system in his approach and actions which merges his agenda of success and his vision. This is something quite unique to Indian polity which has operated more on issues of sublime factors of caste, creed, religion, region and others. Thus in many ways, Narendra Modi has been successful in rising above these factors with voters backing him for his policies, agenda and personality, and not due to some other factors.

He is an adaptive strategic leader, resolute and flexible, persistent in the face of setbacks but also able to strategically react to environmental shifts. Modi is constantly vigilant, understanding the environment and keenly aware of the signals of change. This is how he manages to update his strategy, taking into account changes in the situation and reacting accordingly. Such skills are not needed only in times of growth, but more so when resources are scarce so as to ensure that those resources are focused in the right direction by the right people. Strategic leadership requires the leader to think, act and influence others in ways that promote the enduring success of the organization. Modi understands that in order to effectively influence others, he must understand the impact he has on them. He has used this information to his benefit, being on the ground and talking to them, utilizing technology and social media to be more accessible and looking for the best ways to make him seem like the best candidate. He is one who also understands the needs, styles and motivations of others.

A good leader lays out a strategy that is easy for people to grasp and accept out of trust, and then gets everyone working to work on that strategy. Modi as a leader of the masses clearly lays out his ideas and plans of action, so as to make people aware of the government's plans and hence generate their trust. He is also a long-term strategist, as is indicative from his early years. Several insiders claim that Modi had a knack for forming relationships with leaders who held influence and worked closely with them to learn the tricks of the trade. Driven by his vision of the long-term goal, he seemed to plan his actions and work on what worked best to bring him closer to his goal. This is reflected even now as his role as Prime Minister, when he has been upfront and active in hoping to make close ties with important countries, as part of foreign relations strategy. One such example would be the invitation of various leaders from SAARC countries to his swearing-in ceremony in May 2014. Such leaders also look out for changes and adapt to them. They know that the best strategies are capable of decaying with time and have to be reinvented or renewed from time to time.

A long term strategy aimed at a country's development also requires the leader to take certain actions that would facilitate growth and the achievement of those developmental goals. At a time when companies across the world are looking at China to fulfil their increased manufacturing needs, Modi decided to push India's resources by way of his 'Make in India' initiative, urging companies and investors to consider India as well. Having underutilized labour skills in manufacturing, Modi is also seeking to generate employment within the country and raise the per-capita income and hence, the growth rate. Easier regulations and better infrastructural facilities will help propel investments in this sector, where a majority of the workforce could be employed.

Modi also learns from experience and successful examples. He has taken on such strategies with the aim of building India's economic capability. Taking the example of Japan that follows a more nationalist foreign policy, Modi's recognizes the value of combining investment in economic capability and external strategic capacity. His domestic policy focus is based on understanding a need to revitalize a moribund economy. Such strategic influence is about building commitment to the organization's strategic direction by 'inviting' others into the process; forging relationships and navigating the political landscape. With the recent talks with Japan and China for raising investment in India, Modi managed to get a commitment from them to help raise billions ($20 billion in the next five years). Apart from that, Modi is focusing on a reduction in the recently widening trade imbalance.

Unlike many of his peers, Narendra Modi from day one has displayed and emphasised on global approach. During his tenure as Chief Minister of Gujarat, he ensured that his state remained in the top bracket of foreign investments. He is also a keen learner and observer who displayed a unique quality of learning from others. In his recent visit to Japan as an Indian Prime Minister, he stated that during his tenure as Chief Minister of Gujarat, he would have at least one delegation of Japan every week and he would spend considerable time with them in his quest to understand their ways and ideas.

He has also announced the vision of developing high speed trains with better services and connectivity across India. One of the major promises that Chinese investment holds for India is the railways. India and China have signed a first of its kind agreement for the involvement of Chinese in building and redeveloping railway stations, raising the train speed on several routes to 160 km an hour and also to conduct a feasibility study for high-speed or bullet trains, for its effective and quick implementation. Addressing Indian Americans on his US visit in September, 2014 was a way of making his presence felt, to use the opportunity to connect with more and more people. Such strategies of networking and delivering trust make people look up to leaders.

Strategic thinking involves taking a broad view, involving the right people, understanding information and perspectives, asking probing questions and facilitating conversations. It involves strategizing for the organization or in the case of Modi, the country, to be able to achieve their long-term vision. It also involves taking decisive action, which is precisely where Modi's strength lies.

Footsteps - Chanakya

One of the most prominent examples of a successful leader well-versed with strategy is Chanakya. Indian teacher, philosopher and royal advisor, he is credited to have authored the ancient Indian political treatise *Arthasastra* (Economics). Also identified as Kautilya or Vishnu Gupta, he is considered to be a pioneer in the field of economics and political science, with his work being thought of an important herald to classical economics. *Arthasastra* discusses monetary and fiscal policies, welfare, international relations and war strategies in detail. He also played an important role as a strategic leader to ensure Alexander's defeat when he had attacked India.

Chanakya's strategies on leadership covered a number of aspects including power, punishment and control. These strategies reflect his deep understanding of the people and the world and have become an important guide for leaders across the world. Narendra Modi seems to have learned from Chanakya as well, as he strives to formulate such policies that are inclusive, strategic and would contribute to the development of India. *Chanakya Niti,* through which Chanakya shared his knowledge, covers all aspects of leadership as well as management principles. Modi's thought process and leadership ability is based around Chanakya's lessons, which include various aspects such as self-discipline, control, continuous learning, humility, commitment and determination.

Modi harbours all these qualities, or at least attempts to maintain a balance among these to be an effective leader.

The story of Modi and Chanakya has a great degree of similarity with both being self-made men and taking on the challenges heads-on. It is said that Chanakya displayed a high level of integrity and probity and despite being the sole strategist and reason for decimating the Nanda dynasty, as well as ensuring his student Chandragupta Maurya became king of Magdha, he remained away from any sort of personal gains or benefits. An interesting tale often being told about him is that once a visitor came to meet him during the night while he was doing some official work. The visitor was asked to wait while Chanakya finished his official work, after which Chankaya blew the lamp off and lighted a new lamp while he interacted with the visitor. The visitor asked curiously the reason for blowing off the lamp and then lighting a new lamp, to which Chankaya replied that while he was doing the official work, he was using the lamp and oil which the kingdom has provided him, but as interaction with a personal visitor was not part of his official duty, he is using a lamp and oil which is being paid from his personal pocket. In a similar way, Narendra Modi has been known to be a person of high probity who continuously stresses on the need to maintain an environment which is free from any personal gains for which even his opponents admire him.

Another distinct similarity between Narendra Modi and Chankaya is that of corruption being the main harbinger for them to come to power. While the unprecedented power which led to massive personal and organisational corruption of the last Nanda king Danananda, led to Chankaya (who till then was a teacher in Takshila University) taking on the mantle of warrior waging a war to save India from the clutches of corrupt practices, in Modi's case it was the unprecedented incidents of corruption which led the Indian masses to rally behind him and provide him with a definitive mandate to rule the country. Like master strategists, both combined India into a single thread, desired for change and used the public sentiments coupled with their proven skills in emerging as the leaders of the nation. The only difference is that while Chankaya never ruled the country, for he nurtured his disciple in his student Chandragupta Maurya for the task, Modi took on the mantle as there lies a lot of difference in the needs and aspirations of nations, and due to the difference of systems of governance between a monarchy and democracy.

Chankaya laid great emphasis on rule of the law and on collaborative teamwork for the growth of the nation. One of the major sutra (teachings) of Chankaya Niti is *"Naikya Chakra Paribhramyati"*, which means that as a chariot cannot be drawn by a single wheel, the ruler cannot rule without a team. For good governance and welfare of people, it is important to have a dedicated and diligent team which is committed towards well-being of all the subjects. Narendra Modi has imbibed this philosophy in his governance style and is known to select people based on their commitment to the agenda of growth and their relative strength.

Chankaya was a person of global ambition and has a great knack of geo-political strategy. He knew that during the Greek Invasion in India, the country was no longer confined to its own domestic affairs. In order to maintain peace and harmony, it is important that India poses harmonic tie-ups with Greek generals who were bestowed with their own principalities by Alexander while he returned back to Greece. Sensing such a need, Chankaya ensured marital relationship of Chandragupta Maurya with the daughter of Seleucus Nicator when the latter was defeated by Chandragupta Maurya for control of Taxila and Hindukush region.

Much like the Chankaya's strategy, Narendra Modi has engaged with geo-political powers of his time, namely, China, Japan, SAARC, European Union and USA, and sending across the decisive message of global engagement with them. At the same time, he has also engaged proactively with neighbouring and strategically important countries like Pakistan, Thailand, Bhutan, etc. in order to maintain power and geo-political balance. His most notable balancing of geo-political affairs has been with Japan and Vietnam (of balancing potential challenges from China) and those with Pakistan. Modi thus followed Chankaya Niti to its hilt which always laid emphasis on maintaining strong relationship with powers which might be at rift with one's challengers and competitors in order to keep pressure on one's potential enemy.

Chankaya was known as a masterful political strategist who knew how to spy on the enemy without their knowledge. He never gave in to political tactics by ruthless politicians, similar to how Modi seems to tackle his political opponents. Chanakya focused on a goal-oriented approach, which is what Modi also adopts. Instead of focusing on the problems that exist, he calls for action that needs to be taken in order to overcome those problems. This gives motive to the people and a clear path of action. Although due to his sarcastic streak, he has been known to criticize the previous government for their ways, he looks at action and communicates strategies to the people, where he believes the solution lies.

21 | Initiative

"There are three types of people in this world: those who make things happen, those who watch things happen, and those who wonder what happened."
~ Mary Kay Ash, American businesswoman

The dictionary definition for "initiative" is the action of taking the first step; responsibility for beginning or originating; the characteristic of originating new ideas or methods; the ability to think and act without being urged by another.

Leadership is about taking initiative and positively influencing people around you. It doesn't mean that only people at the top of the rung can start off with a major idea or program. It isn't about position but behaviour and actions. To become a leader one has to start acting like one. Rather than just bringing attention to a problem, a leader starts with a possible solution and liaisons with both his superior and subordinates to solve the problem.

Napoleon Hill, in his book titled *The Law of Success in Sixteen Lessons* states: *"Initiative is the very foundation upon which this necessary quality of Leadership is built. One of the peculiarities of Leadership is the fact that it is never found in those who have not acquired the habit of taking the initiative."*

Initiative is the trait that makes a person stand apart from the crowd and transforms into the leader. It distinguishes a leader because it isn't about following a set of rules or directions but rather finding new ways to do more, to do better. Initiative helps build progress through new and creative methods of accomplishment. It is about being enterprising and having a thrust on action. A lot of people have novel ideas about the world and its problems but only those who dare to act on the idea bring about change and improvement. As John Maxwell said, *"An idea is worthless unless you use it."*

Narendra Modi is one of the most enterprising leaders in the history of India. His Gujarat Model has been praised by all and now he seeks to replicate the success throughout India.

Too dynamic to stick to status quo, Modi has initiated numerous innovative policies and executed them strategically. Leading from the front is something that he does naturally. He has been very successful in selling his ideas to people and firmly believes in the idea that actions speak for themselves. The biennial Vibrant Gujarat Summit has been a huge success in bringing FDI to India. But this wasn't an easy task. He had to overhaul the entire state machinery and was met with resistance on the idea of opening Gujarat up for foreign investment. From inviting multinational companies and foreign entrepreneurs to designing and organizing agricultural festivals and reforming female education, he has done it all to bring about social and economic change that permeates in the form of monetary and non-monetary benefits at all levels of the socio-economic strata.

The right man is the one who seizes the moment." -Johann Wolfgang von Goethe

Showing an eye for identifying opportunity, he offered land at low rates to Ratan Tata to set up a plant at Sanand. Soon, investments poured into Gujarat regularly. He has shown that while making decisions, leaders need to have foresight to envision the future.

Another example of his enterprising ability is The Vadodara Halol Toll project. It is widely cited as the perfect example of the values of 4P - People Public Private Partnership. The concept of 4P is based on Modi's ideology that people are the real beneficiaries of all infrastructure projects and maximum impact can be made if they have a role in design and implementation of the project. Modi ensured public involvement through NGOs, professional groups, local communities and media.

The aforementioned toll project was socially audited. It was noted that the project would require resettlement of about 300 families. To solve the problem, public discussions were carried out. This led to development of several alternatives which reduced the resettlement requirements to only 10 families. The company in charge also voluntarily constructed temples, tools and environmental infrastructure. Rehabilitation measures were also carried out. This project received the designation of the "best practice" project from amongst all the World Bank assisted projects in India.

Now as Prime Minister of India with an overall developmental vision, Modi has created smaller missions to tackle major underlying issues that hamper development. To bring his missions to reality, Modi takes the initiative to set up programs, events and systems that he believes would work to bring about the change. To complement his 'Clean India' campaign, aimed at making every citizen of India aware of the benefits of proper hygiene and sanitation, and to get them to practice it, Modi has decided to hold a World Toilet Summit in New Delhi on November 19, 2014, in association with the World Toilet Organization. This is also an example of how Modi addresses issues plaguing a majority of people, the 'common citizens'. Stating the fact that one major reason for girls' high dropout rates in schools is the lack of proper toilets for them, he insisted that the nation addresses this basic need first. A leader can make elaborate plans and leave them to be followed, but a good leader would supervise the entire process, or at least ensure that someone he trusts would oversee the project and make it work. Modi's mission of a 'Swachh Bharat' by 2019 is one mission he is actively promoting, increasing funds allocated for toilet construction and organizing campaigns to spread awareness.

Modi has also taken the issue of the holy river Ganga on priority and has set up an Inter-Ministerial Group to head the cleaning campaign. Varanasi, the holy city visited by millions of religious Indians, is the base of this operation. Even though the condition of the river has been deplorable despite previous initiatives, that hasn't deterred Modi in planning out the cleanliness drive. In the first phase, the river will be widened by 45 meters and deeper by 3 meters to ferry passengers and goods between Varanasi and Hoogly, along with eleven terminals along the banks of the river.

Narendra Modi has shown that leaders need to lead by example and his hands-on approach has led to his being regarded as the leader who can finally turnaround India and put it on a high growth trajectory.

Footsteps – Franklin D. Roosevelt

"Initiative is doing the right thing without being told.

~Victor Hugo, French writer

Theodore "T.R." Roosevelt, Jr. was an American author, naturalist, explorer, historian, and politician who served as the 26th President of the United States. He was a leader of the Republican Party and founder of the Progressive Party. As a child, Roosevelt suffered from Asthma. To overcome his weakness, he lived a strenuous life. He was a man famous for his exuberant personality and enterprising nature. In his own words, *"It is not often that a man can make opportunities for himself. But he can put himself in such shape that when or if the opportunities come he is ready."*

Roosevelt's enterprising and action-oriented nature is reflected in Modi. Not just this Modi is also similar to Roosevelt in the energy he exudes. Roosevelt became president at a very young age of 42. His energy was contagious he electrified the whole country.

The leaders also share quite a few ideologies. Roosevelt was an outspoken foe of socialism. He believed that capitalism could be preserved with a little restraint and common sense and within months he began to wield his powers and brought about reforms. Modi too seeks to change the fate of the nation through capitalism.

Roosevelt was also a strong personality who never shied away from speaking publically and in fact had quite the knack for it. He spoke with confidence and enthusiasm and was received warmly.

In his famous, speech *The Man In The Arena,* he said, "It is not the critic who counts; not the man who points out how the strong man stumbles, or where the doer of deeds could have done them better. The credit belongs to the man who is actually in the arena, whose face is marred by dust and sweat and blood; who strives valiantly; who errs, who comes short again and again, because there is no effort without error and shortcoming; but who does actually strive to do the deeds; who knows great enthusiasms, the great devotions; who spends himself in a worthy cause; who at the best knows in the end the triumph of high achievement, and who at the worst, if he fails, at least fails while daring greatly, so that his place shall never be with those cold and timid souls who neither know victory nor defeat."

Modi is also a doer and makes sure that he seizes any opportunity that comes his way. His commitments are supported by his actions and his initiatives in most cases have delivered tangible results. This indeed is a rarity in India where most ground political commitments either remain on paper or are shown the light of day in a frail manner.

Roosevelt came at a time when his country was

thirsting for leadership and became a political and popular hero. Narendra Modi too has taken office in an uncannily similar situation.

A leader of uncommon strength, he turned America into a modern superpower through extraordinary will and determination. He led with courage and character and put presidency back as the centre of power in The United States of America.

Narendra Modi too has shown strength of character in his rise to power and one can hope that he will create history like Roosevelt.

ABOUT THE AUTHORS

Nitin Agarwal

Nitin Agarwal is an award winning social entrepreneur who turned down a lucrative corporate career to contribute to the social sector. Through his Foundation 'National Association of School Professionals', he is bringing about a fundamental shift in the way kids are educated in our country. His previous venture 'Chakhle India' was a pleasant change in the way food was consumed and served on Indian roads. An Engineer and MBA (MDI, Gurgaon) by education, he has been widely covered in media for his works.

He can be reached at : *convenor@nasp.in*

Vijay Jhindal

A qualified CA, equipped with an LLB degree, Vijay Jhindal is a multi faceted individual who served as an RSS Pracharak for more than six years, right after his education. While he was serving as Pracharak in Faridabad, Shri Narendra Modi was in charge of ABVP in the state, thus he got a chance to observe him closely and was greatly influenced by his working style especially his outstanding organisational skills.

Mr Jhindal is also a serial entrepreneur with successful forays into Investment Banking, Real Estate, Media, Entertainment and Agriculture.

He can be contacted at : *vkj0077@yahoo.com*
Twitter : @VijayJhindal
Facebook : fb.com/VijayJhindal

Pankaj Sharma

Based out of Boulder, CO, U.S.A, Pankaj Sharma is a social , political and corporate lecturer and commentator. He is an alumni of the pretihious International Visitor's Ledaerhsip Program of the Government of U.S.A and has in past lectured in global universities like Standford, Rice and Naropa. His comments and works regulaly features in global media like Wall Street Journal, New York Times, Cristian Science Monitor, Al Zajeera , Reuters, AFP besides all major Indian media.

He can be reached at : *kaushika.pankaj@gmail.com*